Trading Privilege for
POWER

TRILOGY

Back Cover Book

This is my testimony. This is my discovery: I found God thanks to my time talking to Jesus. I had to make a choice. I chose to forgive. This changed everything. This book is about my spiritual journey of going from being lost and confused to finding purpose and meaning through the loving relationship with Jesus and Athena. This book is about my legal, personal and spiritual discovery. This is my story of who I was, who I am and who I am becoming and a few of the sentinels and stars that helped guide me along the way. I was just a regular Joe then I realized some strange things started happening once I started really asking questions. I asked the best Lawyers to help me and they said they would be happy to help me find answers. This book is an attempt to share what I found with the world. I can breath. I have a voice. (King George VI). I have a lot to share but above all other things nothing is more important than forgiveness and love I found in Tomball TX.

We hold these truths to be self-evident, that all men are created equal, that they are endowed by their Creator with certain unalienable Rights, that among these are Life, Liberty and the pursuit of Happiness.

Preamble to the Declaration of Independence

Preface: by the author, Explains why

we should read the book.

Can 1 person change the world? Some people can some of the time. Can 1 person change their world? Yes they can every time. This is your chance to change your world just like the author changed his. You can love yourself and you can love others. That is what this book is about. The first character Christian struggles to love himself because he doesn't know who he is. He dedicates himself to the noblest cause he can think of which is ending *Racism* through a clever change of the definition. He abolishes the word race from meaning a group of people. A race is a competition. Christian had first hand experience with his civil rights being violated, as a person with a disability, by men who were trying to get ahead and that is what brought him to this realization. His Father, his Pastor and his Trustee took over his life by depriving him all his assets totaling $350,000. They got rich and Christian got Bankrupted. Christian tried but could do nothing about it. He was tortured and felt helpless. He felt suffocated and would wake up in the night gasping for breath. "I CAN'T BREATH." He knew if he hadn't woken up just then it would have been too late and he would have died. He was terrified. He prayed to God to end his life on earth. He couldn't breathe or sleep and the pain was more than he could stand. He wished he had a home to want to go to but his family had abandoned him and left him for dead. Maybe that was their plan all along. He didn't die just then. Somehow he survived. Then he saw the footage of what happened to George Floyd who was suffocated and killed. "HE CAN'T BREATH." Christian saw his face looking for help and answers and justice. Looking at the footage of the murder of Mr. Floyd Christian knew he could have suffered a similar fate but narrowly escaped. Christian believed in both cases a man with power was holding another human back as if they were in a race against each other. Why were they holding Mr. Floyd down like that? Like where was he going to go? For me growing up in professional sports I have seen this before. Sports is a contest. Race is not.

Christian wonders if Father, Pastor, his Trustee, Mother and Mr. J drank up his milkshake with a long straw called a power of attorney?

Jesus knows.

Christian wants to know who paid for the month in Fiji and 5 month vacation to Perth 6 months after his head injury he was in hospital for 12 days and his medical bills were more than $100,000?

Jesus knows who paid for 1 month in Fiji and 5 month vacation to Perth taken 6 months after his head injury?

Christian wants to know why his family was so poor after coming back from that vacation they nearly had to move back to Big Papa's house because his parents had no job, no home and no money and they had just closed up the family charity within a year after Christian's head injury and the vacation.

Preface to the prolog:

Christian is taking full responsibility for his life as well as before and after. Therefore this prologue starts before his journey on earth. He is in that other place. The place we all come from and the place we are all going when this journey is over. Christian takes responsibility for the family he is born into and the circumstances surrounding his upbringing that has played a part in him becoming the person he is today.

PROLOG

This is the beginning of a dream. I just woke up. Here I Am… Here Am I …

As I looked around though, I am not sure where I Am. Or how I got here exactly.

That means I must be, I just fell to sleep.

This must be a dream. This is my dream then and my dream must be controlled by me. This is going to be a nice dream.

What happened before this?

Did it really Happen?

Was all that real?

Does it even matter?

Not really.

Here I AM awake in this dream. Let's have some fun! I want a thrill!!!

A journey in a far off land with a battle to find that could kill me and if i go into it with no way out…

with **The Knowledge** that the journey could *cost me everything* that would be intense! My experiences will seem to be so much more meaningful and seem to be really real if I'm tormented with **The Knowledge** that I have a one way ticket and there's no going back!

So,

This is my dream.

I am born into greatness but rise from nothing too… Like Joseph in the bible. On my journey of failure and success I feel safe and I am safe with dangerous wild women I conquered and others that conquered me. I'm a fighter and a winner. If it were up to me… No. Because it is up to me, I am born into a tradition of greatness. The Glory of sports and entertainment is the birthright I chose. I decided I want my Papa and my Big Papa to be gangsters.

The thing is, now that I'm here I discovered the only way to progress is to take that inherited privilege and sacrifice it. I can't get no; satisfaction from having everything I ordered. I only find peace and happiness once I choose to live a life like Sidhartha. I know in my bones I'm on the path to enlightenment when I see the surender in the eyes of the men and women I conquer - Or when I feel the ecstasy in my heart as I realize what I see is my own reflection in their eyes.

Tomorrow if I'm still in this strange space I have created for myself, friends and enemies, I want to make something else. Something new: Myself. I am; I'm going to be the person with the *prana* I imagined as a child. Although, I don't remember ever being a child… It doesn't matter. I am that person now.

The thrill is I could lose everything and become nothing, or if I'm lucky, integrate one thing and become everything.

BOOK I

A Petition To End The Human Races

Chapter 1

Talk'n to Jesus Podcast:

Jesus

Once again, da hell you talk'n 'bout Christian? He asked in a deep smooth baritone voice.

Christian

Haven't you seen **The Count of Monte Cristo** with **Jim Cavizel?**

"In physics and in man every action has an equal and opposite reaction."

Jesus

Like karma and all that? You know it,

But what are you talk'n bout Christian? What does this really have to do with? You're always talking in riddles when you should just speak your mind. Is this about some female? Or is it about that bull shit from all those years ago I know you're still hung up on with your pastor? Man you have got to stop living in the past and embrace the gift that is the present.

Christian

Jesus Christ I'm trying to but I have so much baggage and its heavy Jesus.

Jesus

Live for today brother. That's all we have any way. I watched a couple of those musicals like you told me I should. Les Mes was good and RENT was dark and dated but good. I get why you like RENT so much but Christian, the whole point of Rent as I see it is there's no day but Today.

Christian

It's about seasons of love and AIDS and heroin and the stages of life and the love we rent from someone for only a period of time.

Jesus

The Musical RENT is about people overcoming the temptation of living in the illusion of the future tragedy of life. Christian, you're the opposite! You have been living in the illusion of the tragedy your life used to be. That's every addict, junkie and alcoholic. That could be your future if you don't get over the past and look to what's coming today. There is no day but today. Live today for your future self. Make a better day today for the person you will be tomorrow. Love that person. It's who you're becoming. The past is only good to learn from and laugh about. Let's talk about something more upbeat. Tell me about your future goals or your past exploits.

Christian

Jesus I'll give it to you. You make some good points. I'm going to have to rethink the meaning of RENT and watch it again. One thing I do know is that circumstances bring people places they never intended to be in musicals myths and in my case. Was my life meant to be like this?

Jesus

Are you actually asking me that?

Christian

Jesus how did I get to a cause of action with Father Pastor Turstee Mother and Mr. J? That's what I mean. Was my life meant to be like this? Then I mean, do you know what I had to do to convince a global law firm to represent me? Not just one guy but the whole company had my back. No contingency, no preconditions. I have a letter of retainer representing me and my cause with a league team league team of the top attorneys so qualified and skilled I don't believe and NFL owner or Billionaire could find better help.

Jesus

Tell me

Christian

All I had to do was ask. I believed I was taken for $10 million. I believed I told them what happened and who I was and I asked.

Jesus

Go on.

Christian

The fact they are based in Minnesota may have helped but a lot of things did... you know my Big Papa's name still has street cred up there.

Jesus

Cm'on now. Stop.

Christian

I didn't call the governor but...

Jesus

Stop it.

Chapter 2
Demand Letter: Fiduciary Accounting

This is what a demand letter looks like. This is polite and frank. It is written to Christian's Father Pastor Trustee and Mr. J. the CFO of for the 501(c)3.

1/12/2020

Via email and CMRRR

Re: Accounting as Fiduciary to ███

Dear Messrs. ███ and ███:

My firm and I represent ███ for purposes of requesting an accounting from you as fiduciaries. A fiduciary relationship may be informal as in a relationship of trust, or formal as with a power of attorney. *See Tex. Bank & Trust Co. v. Moore*, 595 S.W.2d 502, 507-09 (Tex. 1980); *Kinzbach Tool Co. v. Corbett-Wallace Corp.*, 138 Tex. 565, 571 (1942). A person accepts appointment as a power of attorney by "exercising authority or performing duties as an agent..." TEX. ESTATE CODE § 751.022. That person "is a fiduciary" and "has a duty to inform and to account for actions taken under the power of attorney." *Id.* at § 751.101.

An accounting must include:

(1) The property belonging to the principal that has come to the agent's knowledge or into the agent's possession;

(2) Each action taken or decision made by the agent;

(3) A complete account of receipts, disbursements, and other actions of the agent that includes the source and nature of each receipt, disbursement, or action, with receipts of principal and income shown separately;

(4) A listing of all property over which the agent has exercise control that includes:

 (A) An adequate description of each asset; and

 (B) The asset's current value, if the value is known to the agent;

(5) The cash balance on hand and the name and location of the depository at which the cash balance is kept;

(6) Each known liability; and

(7) Any other information and facts known to the agent as necessary for a full and definite understanding of the exact condition of the property belonging to the principal.

Id. at 751.104(b). The fiduciary must also provide "all documentation regarding the principal's property." *Id.* at § 751.104(c). Such documentation shall be provided within 60 days of the date of this request, or we may be forced to "file suit to compel the agent to deliver the accounting" as permitted by the Code. *See id.* at § 751.105(1). A third party who knowingly participates in the fiduciary's breach is a "joint tort-feasor with the fiduciary and is liable as such." *Kinzbach Tool*, 138 Tex. at 574.

This letter serves as notice of revocation of any power of attorney, pursuant to TEXAS ESTATE CODE §§ 751.131(2), 751.132(a)(1).

We look forward to receiving the accounting no later than November 18, 2019, as required by the TEXAS ESTATE CODE. Feel free to contact me to discuss further.

Sincerely,

Chapter 3

ADHD's Mirror NPD

This chapter is left blank intentionally.

The reader should feel free to draw their own conclusions with pictures or words in this chapter. Journaling is helpful. I also recommend reading **Sam Vadkin** who is the best person to inform us about NPD. <u>And *Dirty Laundry: Why Adults with ADHD Are so Ashamed and What We Can Do to Help*</u> by **Richard Pink and Roxane Emery**

Chapter 4

Talk'n to Jesus Podcast:

Christian

Jesus, I want to be honest with you and let you know who I am and what I'm all about. This is where I'm coming from. Jesus, do you know what I did at the company's Christmas party?

Jesus

With that sweet girl from accounts Receivable? Yes of course I do. Or are you talking about the time you met your co-worker's wife at the Christmas party 3 years ago and ended up moving in with her 6 months later? I know about that too. Everyone knows. I want to hear about something most people don't know about you.

Christian

Ok Jesus, let's get down to it. I guess it all started before and after that when I decided to give up all my worldly possessions and follow the spirit just as prescribed very clearly in the New Testament of the Bible.

Jesus

I still can't believe you actually did that Christian. You didn't want anyone at work to know you were homeless sleeping in the back of a 1997 Ford Explorer showering at the gym and trying to keep your clothes organized in the back of that thing where you slept in the Wal-Mart parking lot or any number of places you hoped would be safe. I know a lot of people that have been there and now are doing very well. That is a good place to find out who you are and who you want to be. So tell me, how did you go from sleeping in the back of your Ford to living in a big house with a pool overnight?

Christian

You already know Jesus. Apparently everybody knows but it's an interesting story so for those just turning into the Talk'n To Jesus Podcast here goes. It all started at the company Christmas party a few years ago and one of the guys in Sales told one of the other guys that wives were allowed. Wifes were not allowed, it was just employees for a reason.

Jesus

Go on...

Christian

I was looking for anything real because my entire reality had slipped away like that painting by Munch you know, The Scream. I swear to... well, I mean I swear that painting is about me at this very point in my life. I was falling or maybe flying. I can't call it. The universe had let me down so many ways I wanted to see if it would catch me before I hit the bottom.

Jesus it did. I believed and I received.

Jesus

Are you two still together?

Christian

I lived with her for 2 years and took care of the house and was good to her but now I moved out and we're still good friends today. Her ex-husband and I aren't friends anymore however. He wouldn't explain how to work the pool pumps or surround sound and I think he resented the fact that I thought he would.

Jesus:

Was he into NASCAR?

Christian

Jesus, I'm tired of talking about this. People are going to get the wrong idea about me. I have authored a petition in congress and I want to talk about that. Oh, not to mention I Invited both Royal Homes to join the movement in an open letter.

Jesus

Well hold on if you're not with her who you are with. After all, it's not good for the man to be alone.

Christian

I'm just single. My reality and ego melted away and so how can I be with someone when I'm nobody? Thanks a lot for bringing up the topic of Jesus. It's painful sometimes... but I have a few girls I talk to. All I really want to talk about is my Petition for the people of the United States to end the Human Races. Not the Human Race like *un-aliving* anybody or anything morbid like that, but Human Races because we are one. Hey Jesus, you listened to U2?

Jesus:

Don't change the subject Christian. And you know I'm down with U2, David Bowie, Tori Amos, Bill Nye, The Artist, and and Taylor Swift. Not to mention Ye, and above all 50 Cent because he's the only one who actually became the change he wanted to see in the world. This isn't about me. This is about you buddy. Tell me you have something going with someone you aren't paying like a Barista or stripper of something.

Christian

Cm'on jesus you know that's all i got.

Jesus

Allright son let me hear it.

Christian

Jesus, it's not like that really but I work long hours and bust my ass and it's not like women are looking for good guys to have relationships with so I go to the same bars and coffee shops and I'm friends with the people there so what's wrong with that?

Jesus

Nothing. Absolutely nothing.

Christian

There's this one place you would love called TheThirsTy3 Icehouse. I think it's a Christian place because of the 3 crosses. I drink and eat there and dream and cry about my fucked up life sometines but it doesn't mater because I feel like everyone else there is just like me in some way. It's really strange actually come to think of it.

Jesus

What's her name?

Christian

Lu Ann

Jesus

Oh lord, here we go.

Christian

She's not like the other women. Jesus she's no better than me but no worse. Strangely I mean good bad and ugly but she has the kindest eyes I've ever seen. She's far from perfect but I don't think her kids will ever have to have a financial accounting ordered through the court for possible conversion or breach of fiduciary.

Jesus

Why do you like her like that Christian? What do you really know about her other than you pay her to bring you beer and hamburgers?

Christian

Jesus, after living in my Ford for 90 days I guess I'm like one of those lost boys from Peter Pan looking for something like a woman somewhere between a lover and a mother. I guess I don't have the time or energy to figure out where to look but, yes, the woman brings me beer and food and I love it and her too… I know it's her job to flirt but I like the way she flirts with me and I like the way she makes me feel. I like the person I am and the person I want to become because…

Jesus…
Go on.

Christian

I like the person I imagine I could be if I was with someone like that.

Jesus

I understand that. It's not about who she is, it's about who you are. Because you don't know this person really you can't. Lu Ann you said right? Tell me more about who you think you could be with someone like that.

Christian

I think she's like an angel sometimes and like to imagine her like a goddess.

Jesus

What are you talking about?

Christian

No big deal, just the mother goddess Hathor because she brings me food and is kind.

Jesus

You said she has the kindes eyes. Reminds me of the first time I saw Athena's eyes.

Christian

What happened

Jesus

Listen up. You know Revelation 3:20. You know what that means? Look, you can take this verse and apply it to your game so take notes. The lesson is he doesn't push himself into the house or make any demands. He wont come into her house and put his dirty boots up on the furniture. He won't even take another step unless he is invited to. That said he has made his intention clear. That is what it means to stand at the door and knock.

Behold, I stand at the door and knock. If anyone hears My voice and opens the door, I will come in to him and dine with him, and he with Me.
New King James Version

Christian

How'd that work out for you? I know you're all about love and all that shit is going to get you hurt Jesus. It could get you hurt badly.

Jesus

I know. I used to be a bit naive but Athena opened her door up to me and that changed things.

Christian

I can't believe that worked. Stand at the door and knock. lol

Jesus

Well I learned and grew and now I understand how to go to battle in war if need be. I used to be the just long haired socialist first born son of G. Now I get it thanks to Athena showing me my reflection.

Christian

G?

What was your old man like Jesus? He can't be as bad as mine was. He was a controlling narcissistic SOB. He was a bit of a fundamentalist, you know. Sometimes he would get mad but not just mad I'm talking rage. I also think he was upset because I didn't follow his exact religion. Do you have any idea what that's like Jesus?

Jesus

I'm glad you asked me about this Christian. You told me your pop's was a real gangsta like his father before him first of all and let me tell you mine was truly the OG of all OG's. Yes the Original G. and yes I get it. I get it all. I know how bad it hurt to look to him and ask why he has forsaken me and left me to…

Christin

Die. I felt the same way in College. Dammit Jesus! You son-of-a-bitch. You get it.

Jesus

Sigh

Christian

So what did you do?

Jesus

I forgave them all and now I'm even more popular than he is. Things work themselves out in the end. Athena and her majestic eyes did help ease the pain at first. Tell me more about your Lu Ann and what you see in the windows to her soul.

This podcast ends with
Carry On My Wayward Son
Kansas

Chapter 5

Reply for second Christian's Pastor's Attorney with accounting December 12, 2019 listing total amount from settlement received from settlement before legal fees mines $106,553.10 to show the total cash. **Hedge Fund Gate** received the funds from Christian's Turstee from Christian's account to invest in a free energy company that was going to change the world. **EyeOn America Energy.** All the big names invested in it.

December 12, 2019

Via Electronic Mail to ███

Via Federal Express
███
ATTN ███
███

Re: SECOND REPLY TO YOUR OCTOBER 17, 2019 REQUEST FOR RECORDS REGARDING ███

███

As you are aware from our prior letter as well as emails and phone calls, our firm, The ███, P.C., represents ███ in regard to the above referenced matter. Accordingly, you may direct communications concerning this matter to the undersigned. As previously discussed, we have received and reviewed your letter to ███ and Mr. ███ dated October 17, 2019. ("Your Letter"). As stated in my prior letter dated November 6, 2019 ("Our Letter") as both of our clients are ███ I will refer to ███ and ███ solely for the sake of clarity, by their first names.

As advised in Our Letter, we did not and do not contest ███ duty as a fiduciary to ███ pursuant to the power of attorney issued regarding ███'s finances. As I previously stated and am even more so confident now upon full review of the applicable documents and receiving the whole story, ███ faithfully and appropriately served in his capacity as a fiduciary to ███ and met all applicable fiduciary duties and standards.

available.

    We trust that upon your review of the above provided summary as well as the records provided, you will agree with our position that ▬met all applicable fiduciary duties and standards and that this matter is resolved. Be advised however, if a claim is made against ▬ alleging a breach if any applicable fiduciary standards or obligations, we will vigorously and aggressively oppose any such claims on ▬ behalf. Obviously, that is not a road that we would like to go down, but be advise that we are more than prepared to do so if required. If we need to discuss this letter or the documents provided, please advise and I will be glad to discuss this with you further.

                                          Very truly yours,

cc: ▬ (Sent Via Email)

Attachments:

2002
De La Salle High School Chart of Tuition
Letter from Dr. Mark Steinberg regarding Fees

2003
De La Salle High School Chart of Tuition
Letter from Dr. Mark Steinberg regarding Fees
Receipt from Dr. Mark Steinberg for Portable EEG Machine
Donation Receipt from De La Salle High School for Books Donated
Dental Receipt
Baylor 1098-T (Tuition Statement 2003-2004)

2004
Letter from Dr. Mark Steinberg regarding Fees

Chapter 6

NPD's Shadow BPD

This chapter left blank intentionally. <u>No Plan B for your A Game.</u> The opposite of what to do to create someone who has NPD or BPD, you might say this is the mirror image of the environment that creates and cultivates a person who will develop NPD or BPD. This is also a reminder to be kind when you can with people who may exhibit NPD or BPD traits. They may not have had a parent like Bo Eason. This doesn't excuse bad behavior but maybe we can be understanding and graceful with others with their own unique struggles.

Chapter 7

Talk'n to Jesus Podcast:

The circles Jesus runs in people see the story of Joseph and his coat a man lost and loves Potiphar's wife but like a boy loves his mother and she lies about him after he turns her down. The the brothers are guilty when they say they should be blamed it's because they put the cup in Benjamin's bag not Joseph.

Jesus:

What is all this?

Christian: It's not easy to talk about but it looks like th same amount of money my pastor my father and my trustee and his friend were allowed to manage for my benefit is the same amount of money that went through their non-taxable company during the exact years they were in charge of it.

Jesus:
What are you saying Christian?

Christian
Jesus can we talk about something else less painful like the fact that we divide people up in groups called Races. It's like we have no chance of living happy together as a Human Race so I petitioned the people of the United States through congress to end the Human Races declaring that it is unlawful to use the word race like that. It may as well be the worst hate speech ever invented.

Jesus
That's less painful than talking about your family business because I see you stare off like you might be still thinking human races or about Lu Ann?

Christian
Jusus Christ, I just feel like I'm autistic sometimes and don't communicate what I want the way I want. I tell her this and that but she doesn't hear it. I don't know what she hears but I do know what I see in her eyes gives me wings or more like I don't need wings. It's hard to explain but I'm sure you get it; like with Athena being your mirror I think her eyes are windows to her soul or they are mirrors and windows. I can't tell if that's her soul through the window or mine reflection off the mirror. What I do know is

I'm addicted.

Jesus

If you have something to say just say it plainly Christian. Your ENERGY (POWER) is scattered.

Christian

I'm sure it is. Just like this one like the rising and setting of the sun. I don't know if it's me or her that is like the rising and setting of the sun but i think it's her. Like Ra or a Little Horus but always she is Hathor giving birth to my Inspiration.

Jesus

Well women motivate men and men can motivate women to do all sorts of things. What does this one motivate you to do?

Christian

To be the best version of myself. The person I see when I look and imagine who I could be with the person I imagine she is.

Jesus

I can dig it.

Chapter 8
990 Tax returns

If you add up the total cash donations the nonprofit it is within $117.00 dollars of the exact amount Christian's Pastor-Father was trusted with for Christian's benefit. After subtracting the $106,553.10 Pastor Father Trustee spent on league fees per fiduciary accounting dated December 12, 2019 sent to Christian's attorney by Christian's Pastor Father and Trustee.

Almost all that money went to Christian's Mother as salary as listed in the 990's signed by all officers and filed with the IRS and The Secretary of The State of California.

State of California
Kevin Shelley
Secretary of State

STATEMENT OF INFORMATION
(Domestic Nonprofit Corporation)

Filing Fee $20.00 — If Amendment, See Instructions

IMPORTANT — READ INSTRUCTIONS BEFORE COMPLETING THIS FORM

04-728575

FILED
in the office of the Secretary of State
of the State of California

OCT 0 4 2004

KEVIN SHELLEY, SECRETARY OF STATE

1. CORPORATE NAME: ~~International~~ Sports ~~~~ C 1918607
   631 Silver Lake Dr
   Danville CA 94526
   Entity ID Corp 1918607

2. STREET ADDRESS OF PRINCIPAL OFFICE IN CALIFORNIA: 631 Silver Lake Drive — CITY: Danville — STATE: CA — ZIP: 94526

3. MAILING ADDRESS:

NAMES AND COMPLETE ADDRESSES OF THE FOLLOWING OFFICERS:

4. CHIEF EXECUTIVE OFFICER / [redacted] — ADDRESS [redacted] — CITY AND STATE: Danville CA — ZIP: 94526
5. SECRETARY / [redacted] — ADDRESS [redacted] — CITY AND STATE: Danville CA — ZIP: 94526
6. CHIEF FINANCIAL OFFICER / [redacted] — ADDRESS [redacted] — CITY AND STATE: Danville CA — ZIP: 94506

AGENT FOR SERVICE OF PROCESS

7. [X] AN INDIVIDUAL RESIDING IN CALIFORNIA.
   [ ] A CORPORATION WHICH HAS FILED A CERTIFICATE PURSUANT TO CALIFORNIA CORPORATIONS CODE SECTION 1505.
   AGENT'S NAME: [redacted]

8. ADDRESS OF THE AGENT FOR SERVICE OF PROCESS IN CALIFORNIA: 631 Silver Lake Drive — CITY: Danville — STATE: CA — ZIP: 94526

DAVIS-STIRLING COMMON INTEREST DEVELOPMENT ACT

9. [ ] CHECK HERE IF THE CORPORATION IS AN ASSOCIATION FORMED TO MANAGE A COMMON INTEREST DEVELOPMENT UNDER THE DAVIS-STIRLING COMMON INTEREST DEVELOPMENT ACT AND PROCEED TO ITEMS 10, 11, 12 AND 13.

10. ADDRESS OF BUSINESS OR CORPORATE OFFICE OF THE ASSOCIATION, IF ANY

11. FRONT STREET AND NEAREST CROSS STREET FOR THE PHYSICAL LOCATION OF THE COMMON INTEREST DEVELOPMENT

12. NAME AND ADDRESS OF ASSOCIATION'S MANAGING AGENT, IF ANY

13. [ ] CHECK HERE IF THE ASSOCIATION'S MANAGING AGENT IS CERTIFIED PURSUANT TO BUSINESS AND PROFESSIONS CODE SECTION 11502.

14. THE INFORMATION CONTAINED HEREIN IS TRUE AND CORRECT.

[redacted signature] — TITLE: Secretary — DATE: 10-1-04

SI-100 (REV-2 01/2003)

04-728575

International Sports Leadership Direc

San Jose, CA 95120

Santa Cruz, CA 95062

Burlingame, CA 94010

Danville, CA 94506

Poway, CA 92064

Birmingham, AL 35243

Raleigh, NC 27614

N. Barrington, IL 60010

Woodbury, MN 55125

Danville, CA 94526

Danville, CA 94526

State of California
Secretary of State
STATEMENT OF INFORMATION 102
(Domestic Nonprofit Corporation)

N 06-719956

Filing Fee $20.00. If amendment, see instructions.

IMPORTANT — READ INSTRUCTIONS BEFORE COMPLETING THIS FORM

1. CORPORATE NAME (Please do not alter if name is preprinted.)

C1918607 RE NCD
███████████ SPORTS L███████████
631 SILVER LAKE DR
DANVILLE CA 94526

FILED
In the office of the Secretary of State
of the State of California

OCT 1 0 2006

DUE DATE: 12-31-06

COMPLETE PRINCIPAL OFFICE ADDRESS (Do not abbreviate the name of the city. Item 2 cannot be a P.O. Box.)

2. STREET ADDRESS OF PRINCIPAL OFFICE IN CALIFORNIA, IF ANY: 631 Silver Lake Drive | CITY: Danville | STATE: CA | ZIP CODE: 94526

NAMES AND COMPLETE ADDRESSES OF THE FOLLOWING OFFICERS (The corporation must have these three officers. A comparable title for the specific officer may be added, however, the preprinted titles on this form must not be altered.)

3. CHIEF EXECUTIVE OFFICER/ ███████ | ADDRESS: ███ Silver Lake Dr | CITY AND STATE: Danville CA | ZIP CODE: 94526
4. SECRETARY/ ███████ | ADDRESS: 631 Silver Lake Dr | CITY AND STATE: Danville CA | ZIP CODE: 94526
5. CHIEF FINANCIAL OFFICER/ ███████ | ADDRESS: ███████████ Dr | CITY AND STATE: Danville CA | ZIP CODE: 94506

AGENT FOR SERVICE OF PROCESS (If the agent is an individual, the agent must reside in California and Item 7 must be completed with a California address. If the agent is another corporation, the agent must have on file with the California Secretary of State a certificate pursuant to Corporations Code section 1505 and Item 7 must be left blank.)

6. NAME OF AGENT FOR SERVICE OF PROCESS: ███████

7. ADDRESS OF AGENT FOR SERVICE OF PROCESS IN CALIFORNIA, IF AN INDIVIDUAL: 631 Silver Lake Dr | CITY: Danville | STATE: CA | ZIP CODE: 94526

DAVIS-STIRLING COMMON INTEREST DEVELOPMENT ACT (California Civil Code section 1350, et seq.)

8. ☐ Check here if the corporation is an association formed to manage a common interest development under the Davis-Stirling Common Interest Development Act and proceed to Items 9, 10 and 11.

NOTE: Corporations formed to manage a common interest development must also file a Statement by Common Interest Development Association (Form SI-CID) as required by California Civil Code section 1363.6. Please see instructions on the reverse side of this form.

9. ADDRESS OF BUSINESS OR CORPORATE OFFICE OF THE ASSOCIATION, IF ANY | CITY | STATE | ZIP CODE

10. FRONT STREET AND NEAREST CROSS STREET FOR THE PHYSICAL LOCATION OF THE COMMON INTEREST DEVELOPMENT | 9-DIGIT ZIP CODE
(Complete if the business or corporate office is not on the site of the common interest development.)

11. NAME AND ADDRESS OF ASSOCIATION'S MANAGING AGENT, IF ANY | CITY | STATE | ZIP CODE

12. THE INFORMATION CONTAINED HEREIN IS TRUE AND CORRECT.

TITLE: Secretary | DATE: 10-5-06

SI-100 (REV 07/2006)

Schedule A (Form 990 or 990-EZ) 2007 INTERNATIONAL SPORTS LEADERSHIP   68-0344971   Page 4

Part IV-A Support Schedule (Complete only if you checked a box on line 10, 11, or 12.) Use cash method of accounting.

Note: You may use the worksheet in the instructions for converting from the accrual to the cash method of accounting.

Calendar year (or fiscal year beginning in)	(a) 2006	(b) 2005	(c) 2004	(d) 2003	(e) Total
15 Gifts, grants, and contributions received. (Do not include unusual grants. See line 28.)	44,458.	41,242.	51,680.	51,624.	189,004.
16 Membership fees received					0.
17 Gross receipts from admissions, merchandise sold or services performed, or furnishing of facilities in any activity that is related to the organization's charitable, etc, purpose					0.
18 Gross income from interest, dividends, amts rec'd from payments on securities loans (sec. 512(a)(5)), rents, royalties, income from similar sources, and unrelated business taxable income (less sec. 511 taxes) from businesses acquired by the organization after June 30, 1975					0.
19 Net income from unrelated business activities not included in line 18					0.
20 Tax revenues levied for the organization's benefit and either paid to it or expended on its behalf					0.
21 The value of services or facilities furnished to the organization by a governmental unit without charge. Do not include the value of services or facilities generally furnished to the public without charge					0.
22 Other income. Attach a schedule. Do not include gain or (loss) from sale of capital assets					0.
23 Total of lines 15 through 22	44,458.	41,242.	51,680.	51,624.	189,004.
24 Line 23 minus line 17	44,458.	41,242.	51,680.	51,624.	189,004.
25 Enter 1% of line 23	445.	412.	517.	516.	

26 Organizations described on lines 10 or 11: a Enter 2% of amount in column (e), line 24 .... N/A .... ▶ 26a

b Prepare a list for your records to show the name of and amount contributed by each person (other than a governmental unit or publicly supported organization) whose total gifts for 2003 through 2006 exceeded the amount shown in line 26a. Do not file this list with your return. Enter the total of all these excess amounts .... ▶ 26b

c Total support for section 509(a)(1) test: Enter line 24, column (e) .... ▶ 26c

d Add: Amounts from column (e) for lines: 18 _____ 19 _____
 22 _____ 26b _____ ▶ 26d

e Public support (line 26c minus line 26d total) .... ▶ 26e

f Public support percentage (line 26e (numerator) divided by line 26c (denominator)) .... ▶ 26f   %

27 Organizations described on line 12:

a For amounts included in lines 15, 16, and 17 that were received from a 'disqualified person,' prepare a list for your records to show the name of, and total amounts received in each year from, each 'disqualified person.' Do not file this list with your return. Enter the sum of such amounts for each year:

(2006) _____ 32,290. (2005) _____ 24,872. (2004) _____ 41,973. (2003) _____ 32,074.

b For any amount included in line 17 that was received from each person (other than 'disqualified persons'), prepare a list for your records to show the name of, and amount received for each year, that was more than the larger of (1) the amount on line 25 for the year or (2) $5,000. (Include in the list organizations described in lines 5 through 11b, as well as individuals.) Do not file this list with your return. After computing the difference between the amount received and the larger amount described in (1) or (2), enter the sum of these differences (the excess amounts) for each year:

(2006) _____ 0. (2005) _____ 0. (2004) _____ 0. (2003) _____ 0.

c Add: Amounts from column (e) for lines: 15 _____ 189,004. 16 _____
 17 _____ 20 _____ 21 _____ ▶ 27c 189,004.

d Add: Line 27a total _____ 131,209. and line 27b total _____ 0. ▶ 27d 131,209.

e Public support (line 27c total minus line 27d total) .... ▶ 27e 57,795.

f Total support for section 509(a)(2) test: Enter amount from line 23, column (e) ▶ 27f 189,004.

g Public support percentage (line 27e (numerator) divided by line 27f (denominator)) .... ▶ 27g 30.58 %

h Investment income percentage (line 18, column (e) (numerator) divided by line 27f (denominator)) .... ▶ 27h 0. %

28 Unusual Grants: For an organization described in line 10, 11, or 12 that received any unusual grants during 2003 through 2006, prepare a list for your records to show, for each year, the name of the contributor, the date and amount of the grant, and a brief description of the nature of the grant. Do not file this list with your return. Do not include these grants in line 15.

2007   FEDERAL STATEMENTS   PAGE 1

███████ SPORTS ███████   68-0344971

STATEMENT 1
FORM 990, PART II, LINE 43
OTHER EXPENSES

	(A) TOTAL	(B) PROGRAM SERVICES	(C) MANAGEMENT & GENERAL	(D) FUNDRAISING
BOOKS PUBLISHING	1,606.	1,606.		
DUES AND SUBSCRIPTIONS	110.	105.	5.	
INTERNET SERVICE	239.	227.	12.	
LICENSES AND FEES	125.	119.	6.	
MEALS AND ENTERTAINMENT	12.	12.		
PROGRAM EXPENSES	551.	551.		
TOTAL	$ 2,643.	$ 2,620.	$ 23.	$ 0.

STATEMENT 2
FORM 990, PART III
ORGANIZATION'S PRIMARY EXEMPT PURPOSE

TO PROVIDE CHRISTIAN MINISTRY TO SPORTS LEADERS.

STATEMENT 3
FORM 990, PART III, LINE A
STATEMENT OF PROGRAM SERVICE ACCOMPLISHMENTS

DESCRIPTION	GRANTS AND ALLOCATIONS	PROGRAM SERVICE EXPENSES
███████ SPORTS ███████ IS A CHRISTIAN MINISTRY DEDICATED TO EVANGELISM AND DISCIPLESHIP OF INTERNATIONAL SPORTS LEADERS AND SPORTS INFLUENCERS. WE FORM A PARTNERSHIP WITH THESE LEADERS TO OPEN DOORS FOR MINISTRY AROUND THE WORLD BY PERSONAL MEETINGS, SMALL GROUP BIBLE STUDIES AND TEACHING AT PROFESSIONAL CONFERENCES. WE HELP LEADERS GROW AS CHRISTIANS IN THEIR PROFESSIONAL LIVES. WE ALSO SEND OUT A WEEKLY DEVOTION VIA THE INTERNET TO STRENGTHEN MARRIAGES AND FAMILY LIFE.		
THE MINISTRY SPENDS TIME IN THE DEVELOPMENT OF TRUSTING AND CLOSE RELATIONSHIPS WITH PROFESSIONAL SPORTS FAMILIES THROUGH HOSPITALITY AND FELLOWSHIP, WITH THE PURPOSE OF MINISTERING TO THEIR SPIRITUAL NEEDS. INCLUDES FOREIGN GRANTS: NO		26,595.
	$ 0.	$ 26,595.

2007 FEDERAL STATEMENTS PAGE 2
                                                                68-0344971

STATEMENT 4
FORM 990, PART IV, LINE 57
LAND, BUILDINGS, AND EQUIPMENT

CATEGORY	BASIS	ACCUM. DEPREC.	BOOK VALUE
FURNITURE AND FIXTURES	$ 1,246.	$ 1,246.	$ 0.
MACHINERY AND EQUIPMENT	1,477.	1,426.	51.
TOTAL	$ 2,723.	$ 2,672.	$ 51.

STATEMENT 5
FORM 990, PART V-A
LIST OF OFFICERS, DIRECTORS, TRUSTEES, AND KEY EMPLOYEES

NAME AND ADDRESS	TITLE AND AVERAGE HOURS PER WEEK DEVOTED	COMPEN- SATION	CONTRI- BUTION TO EBP & DC	EXPENSE ACCOUNT/ OTHER
	PRESIDENT 5.00	$ 0.	$ 0.	$ 0.
	SECRETARY 30.00	28,500.	0.	0.
	BOARD MEMBER 1.00	0.	0.	0.
	BOARD MEMBER 1.00	0.	0.	0.
	BOARD MEMBER 1.00	0.	0.	0.
	BOARD MEMBER 1.00	0.	0.	0.
	BOARD MEMBER 1.00	0.	0.	0.
	BOARD MEMBER 1.00	0.	0.	0.
	BOARD MEMBER 1.00	0.	0.	0.

2007 FEDERAL STATEMENTS PAGE 3
███████ SPORTS ███████ 68-0344971

STATEMENT 5 (CONTINUED)
FORM 990, PART V-A
LIST OF OFFICERS, DIRECTORS, TRUSTEES, AND KEY EMPLOYEES

NAME AND ADDRESS	TITLE AND AVERAGE HOURS PER WEEK DEVOTED	COMPEN-SATION	CONTRI-BUTION TO EBP & DC	EXPENSE ACCOUNT/ OTHER
BILL HARGIS 1288 KENILWORTH WOODBURY, MN 55125	BOARD MEMBER 1.00	$ 0.	$ 0.	$ 0.
	TOTAL	$ 28,500.	$ 0.	$ 0.

STATEMENT 6
FORM 990, PART V-A, LINE 75C
INDIVIDUALS COMPENSATION BY RELATED ORGANIZATIONS

RELATED ORGANIZATION: SPORTS LEADERSHIP GROUP
FEIN: 20-1473110
RELATIONSHIP EXPLANATION: ███████ IS THE PRESIDENT OF IN███████ SPORTS ███████ AND ███████ IS ALSO WIFE, IS SECRETARY. ███████ PRESIDENT AND A SHAREHOLDER OF SPORTS LEADERSHIP GROUP, A FOR-PROFIT CORPORATION. ███████ IS SECRETARY OF SPORTS ███████ BOTH AND ███████ ARE EMPLOYEES OF SPORTS ███████ GROUP.

COMPENSATION PAID: $ 63,946.
BENEFIT PLAN CONTRIBUTIONS: $ 0.
EXPENSE ACCOUNT: $ 0.
COMPENSATION ARRANGEMENT: SPORTS ███████ PAID ███████ WAGES OF $63,946. ███████ SPORTS ███████ PAID ███████ WAGES OF $-0-. ███████ SPORTS ███████ PAID ███████ WAGES OF $28,500

2007 FEDERAL BOOK DEPRECIATION SCHEDULE

6/30/08
FORM 990/990-PF — SPORTS
68-0344971
PAGE 1

NO.	DESCRIPTION	DATE ACQUIRED	DATE SOLD	COST/ BASIS	BUS PCT	CUR 179 BONUS	SPECIAL DEPR. ALLOW.	PRIOR 179/ BONUS/ SP DEPR	PRIOR DEC BAL DEPR	SALVAG /BASIS REDUCT	DEPR. BASIS	PRIOR DEPR	METHOD	LIFE	RATE	CURRENT DEPR
	FURNITURE AND FIXTURES															
1	OFFICE EQUIPMENT - DESK	7/01/95		1,246			0	0	0	0	1,246	1,246	S/L	7		0
	TOTAL FURNITURE AND FIXTURE			1,246			0	0	0	0	1,246	1,246				0
	MACHINERY AND EQUIPMENT															
2	DELL COMPUTER	12/18/03		1,477			0	0	0	0	1,477	1,131	S/L	5		295
	TOTAL MACHINERY AND EQUIPME			1,477			0	0	0	0	1,477	1,131				295
	TOTAL DEPRECIATION			2,723			0	0	0	0	2,723	2,377				295
	GRAND TOTAL DEPRECIATION			2,723			0	0	0	0	2,723	2,377				295

Form 990-EZ (2008) INTERNATIONAL SPORTS LEADERSHIP 68-0344971 Page 2

Part III Statement of Program Service Accomplishments (See the instructions.)

What is the organization's primary exempt purpose? SEE STATEMENT 3

Describe what was achieved in carrying out the organization's exempt purposes. In a clear and concise manner, describe the services provided, the number of persons benefited, or other relevant information for each program title

Expenses (Required for 501(c)(3) and (4) organizations and 4947(a)(1) trusts; optional for others)

28 SEE STATEMENT 4

(Grants $_____) If this amount includes foreign grants, check here ▶ ☐ | 28a | 12,913.

29 _____

(Grants $_____) If this amount includes foreign grants, check here ▶ ☐ | 29a |

30 _____

(Grants $_____) If this amount includes foreign grants, check here ▶ ☐ | 30a |

31 Other program services (attach schedule)

(Grants $_____) If this amount includes foreign grants, check here ▶ ☐ | 31a |

32 Total program service expenses (add lines 28a through 31a) ▶ | 32 | 12,913.

Part IV List of Officers, Directors, Trustees, and Key Employees. (List each one even if not compensated. See the instrs.)

(a) Name and address	(b) Title and average hours per week devoted to position	(c) Compensation (if not paid, enter -0-.)	(d) Contributions to employee benefit plans and deferred compensation	(e) Expense account and other allowances
[redacted] MAGNOLIA, TX 77354	PRESIDENT 5.00	0.	0.	0.
[redacted] MAGNOLIA, TX 77354	SECRETARY 30.00	13,500.	0.	0.
[redacted] 1544 CAROL AVE BURLINGAME, CA 94010	BOARD MEMBER 1.00	0.	0.	0.
[redacted] 6883 GOLDPINE CT SAN JOSE, CA 95120	BOARD MEMBER 1.00	0.	0.	0.
[redacted] 734 EL PINTADO RD DANVILLE, CA 94506	BOARD MEMBER 1.00	0.	0.	0.
[redacted] 1030 IMAGES SQUARE CROPWELL, AL 35054	BOARD MEMBER 1.00	0.	0.	0.
[redacted] 2309 NARRAWOOD ST RALEIGH, NC 27614	BOARD MEMBER 1.00	0.	0.	0.

BAA TEEA0812L 01/14/09 Form 990-EZ (2008)

Schedule A (Form 990 or 990-EZ) 2008 INTERNATIONAL SPORTS LEADERSHIP   68-0344971   Page 3

Part III | Support Schedule for Organizations Described in Section 509(a)(2)
(Complete only if you checked the box on line 9 of Part I.)

Section A. Public Support

Calendar year (or fiscal yr beginning in) ►	(a) 2004	(b) 2005	(c) 2006	(d) 2007	(e) 2008	(f) Total
1 Gifts, grants, contributions and membership fees received. (Do not include 'unusual grants.')	51,680.	41,242.	44,458.	33,633.	19,986.	190,999.
2 Gross receipts from admissions, merchandise sold or services performed, or facilities furnished in a activity that is related to the organization's tax-exempt purpose						0.
3 Gross receipts from activities that are not an unrelated trade or business under section 513						0.
4 Tax revenues levied for the organization's benefit and either paid to or expended on its behalf						0.
5 The value of services or facilities furnished by a governmental unit to the organization without charge						0.
6 Total. Add lines 1-5	51,680.	41,242.	44,458.	33,633.	19,986.	190,999.
7a Amounts included on lines 1, 2, 3 received from disqualified persons	41,973.	24,872.	32,290.	21,718.	1,006.	121,859.
b Amounts included on lines 2 and 3 received from other than disqualified persons that exceed the greater of 1% of the total of lines 9, 10c, 11, and 12 for the year or $5,000	0.	0.	0.	0.	0.	0.
c Add lines 7a and 7b	41,973.	24,872.	32,290.	21,718.	1,006.	121,859.
8 Public support (Subtract line 7c from line 6.)						69,140.

Section B. Total Support

Calendar year (or fiscal yr beginning in) ►	(a) 2004	(b) 2005	(c) 2006	(d) 2007	(e) 2008	(f) Total
9 Amounts from line 6	51,680.	41,242.	44,458.	33,633.	19,986.	190,999.
10a Gross income from interest, dividends, payments received on securities loans, rents, royalties and income form similar sources						0.
b Unrelated business taxable income (less section 511 taxes) from businesses acquired after June 30, 1975.						0.
c Add lines 10a and 10b	0.	0.	0.	0.	0.	0.
11 Net income from unrelated business activities not included in line 10b, whether or not the business is regularly carried on						0.
12 Other income. Do not include gain or loss from the sale of capital assets (Explain in Part IV.)						0.
13 Total support. (add ins 9, 10c, 11, and 12.)						190,999.

14 First five years. If the Form 990 is for the organization's first, second, third, fourth, or fifth tax year as a section 501(c)(3) organization, check this box and stop here ► ☐

Section C. Computation of Public Support Percentage

15 Public support percentage for 2008 (line 8, column (f) divided by line 13, column (f))	15	36.2 %
16 Public support percentage from 2007 Schedule A, Part IV-A, line 27g	16	30.6 %

Section D. Computation of Investment Income Percentage

17 Investment income percentage for 2008 (line 10c, column (f) divided by line 13, column (f))	17	0.0 %
18 Investment income percentage from 2007 Schedule A, Part IV-A, line 27h	18	0.0 %

19a 33-1/3 support tests — 2008. If the organization did not check the box on line 14, and line 15 is more than 33-1/3%, and line 17 is not more than 33-1/3%, check this box and stop here. The organization qualifies as a publicly supported organization ► ☒

b 33-1/3 support tests — 2007. If the organization did not check a box on line 14 or 19a, and line 16 is more than 33-1/3%, and line 18 is not more than 33-1/3%, check this box and stop here. The organization qualifies as a publicly supported organization ► ☐

20 Private foundation. If the organization did not check a box on line 14, 19a, or 19b, check this box and see instructions ► ☐

BAA   TEEA0403L 01/29/09   Schedule A (Form 990 or 990-EZ) 2008

Chapter 9

Atlas Shrugged

A great book talks about personal property and obtaining money from the work you do rather than taking it by force from some and giving it to others because they may seem more deserving. This is an intentional illusion to how Christian's pastor took his money and refused to return it or dividends from his company started with that money because he thought that was somehow the right thing to do.

This chapter contains blank pages for the reader to draw their own conclusions with pictures or words.

Chapter 10

Christian's Inspiration

The 990's hit like William Wallace realizing his friend betrayed him only **100x worse.** All that money that went into the charity went out to pay his own mother in salary while he was suffocating.

Chcristian left the desert. He had nothing and was nobody. That is what happens in the desert. What can bring us out of the desert? A dream? An Angel? God? Jesus? These are tools and symbolic representations to describe a tool of inspiration. Christian is inspired. Inspiration is first in every endeavor. 40 years or 40 days, wherever you are it is there. It is everywhere and all around us. In the desert experience you lose everything so you can find anything. This is the start of something. This is the start of everything. It already is the start of something good for you.

Like that poem or quote, by F. Scott Fitzgerled:

"For what it's worth... it's never too late, or in my case too early to be whoever you want. You can change or stay the same. There are no rules to this thing. We can make the best or the worst of it. I hope you make the best of it. I hope you see things that startle you. I hope you feel things

you've never felt before. I hope you meet people who have a different point of view. I hope you live a life you're proud of, and if you're not, I hope you have the courage to start over again."

Without inspiration you stay in the desert and in the past reliving the tragedy your life used to be and only is still because you stayed in the desert. Christian still has a lot to learn from Jesus but they are on the same path just at different points. Christian is looking for Information now that he has found his Inspiration and overcomes the temptation of staying in the desert, but he still knows nothing about who he is or who anybody else is. This makes it impossible to have any meaningful connection with anyone. Without any meaningful connection with himself or anyone else information is worthless. Of course that is the one thing he is seeking now since leaving the isolation of the desert. Thank god he has Jesus and Athena.

Now back to Christian at TheThirsTy3 ICEHOUSE. He could be in any town in the world and have this same experience. It is the most important experience one can have and the conditions to create this experience are all around any and everyone every day. It is no different from The Great Buddha finding enlightenment there under that tree after going through the desert of his heart and mind. Christin has given up all his possessions, friends and family to get to the source.

Who am I? Where am I? Why am I here? He had the strength to ask those questions and was brave enough to accept the answer. This is what happened to Christian in the beginning and in the end. After a long hard day at work he was sitting on a bar stool at TheThirsTy3. He looks up and he sees who he is in the eyes of Lu Ann who appears to be the mother goddess of Egypt. Hathor flashes the eyes of Ra and Horus. Any baggage he had left from wandering in the desert was consumed in the rising and setting sun in her eyes. A person he hardly knows but he hardly knows the person he is so it makes for a perfect match. Now he can be reborn because all the junk and of the person he was is gone. This is the happiest and the saddest day of his life. Happy because he was a new person. The person with the prana he always wanted to be. The saddest because he was more alone than ever even when he was in the desert. As a new person now nobody knew who he was. No one but Lu Ann.

Trading Privilege

for

POWER

TRILOGY

BOOK II

Information

By:

Joseph G. Black

Chapter 1

The Listening to Jesus Podcast

Jesus says:

I am.

I am who?

I am Who I am.

I am Who? - I am.

I am who I am and that is exactly who I am meant to be today.
I am who I am and that is enough for today.

I am loved.

I am who I love.

I am loved by who I am.

I am who loves my body; It has taken me this far.

I am who loves my mind; it gives me understanding.

I am that person that can say who loves my soul; it shows me how to treat others and myself.

I create my reality thanks to the state of my body, mind and soul.

I take responsibility for who I have become and who I will be.

I take responsibility for how others treat me now that I am.

I am Awake? Who are you?

Wake up!
Wake up!
Wake up!

I AM. Who woke up.

I show the universe what I will and will not tolerate.

I Am Who I Am.

Thankful.

Grateful.

Respectful.

For me and those all around me.

For the day I made. And the day I can make.

Of this journey, in this far off land.

(Suddenly Christian opens the door to the Podcast room and interrupts Jesus.)

...Said Christian.

Jesus says:
...I am happy. I am blessed. I have everything I want and more than I, *"Christian sit down and wait,"* need.

(Jesus takes a deep breath inhales through his nose slowly counting to 4. Holds his breath counting slowly to 4. Slowly exhales through his mouth counting slowly to 4.)

Jesus says:

God, grant me the strength to forgive. The courage to be generous. And the wisdom to know I am free.

(Jesus takes a deep breath inhales through his nose slowly counting to 4. Holds his breath counting slowly to 4. Slowly exhales through his mouth counting slowly to 4.)

Jesus says:

I'm glad you arrived early today Christian.

… Said Christian.

Jesus says:

Some people call it meditation. Some call it prayer. I call it focus.

... Said Christian.

Jesus says:

Every day I take time to remember the truth. I mean, I have to remind myself of the reality I live in; what is true will set you free!

... Said Christian.

Jesus says:

The truth is I can do anything I choose; I can have anything I want as long as I remember: I am Who I am.

This isn't the first time you heard this Christian however you may not realize it. All the secret knowledge you seek you have already been told but didn't hear it.   *(Phillipians 4:13)* **13** *I can do all things through [a]Christ who strengthens me.*

... Said Christian.

Jesus says:

Not everything you heard in Sunday school is a lie Christian. They never explain this one very well so, *I'll help you download the update.*

Christ is in all of us. No, not the Jewish zealot but when it says Christ here, it means that thing that is in all of us that Yeshua was in touch with within himself. Some call it the higher self but it is the combination of the higher and lower self in total integration. It is the true self. The one self which is the higher self to those looking in from outside.

... Said Christian.

Jesus says:

I can see I have confused you. Christ is used as a metaphor for the Ubermensch that is in all of us!

... Said Christian.

Jesus says:

Any way, the day I found The Truth (Veritas,) I promised to who I Am, I wouldn't ever forget it.

This is why I take time every morning afternoon and night to stop everything all around outside and inside to remember this one thing.

... Said Christian.

Jesus says:

Exactly like like, and definitely not like your favorite Sci-Fi.. uh, is Lord Of The... Sci-Fi?

... Said Christian.

Jesus says:

You're asking if women ever love the nice honest guy or just always pick the dishonest bad-guy?

(All the things we can talk about and you want to talk about this.)

Ok. First of all you sound bitter Christian like your mind is clouded with envy? Or worse, you may have anger and hate in your heart which will make you unable to see the truth or hear what I'm about to tell you.

The Truth is going to be hard for you to hear and even harder for you to accept Christian.

The Veritas is, they want you.

Doesn't matter if you're nice or mean, or a winner or a loser. They want you. Your problem is Christian, you don't know who you are?

... Said Christian.

Jesus says:
So you were nice to a girl and she didn't choose you? She chose a shallow

careless boy who doesn't respect her? Well that's no surprise to me Christian. It has nothing to do with your looks, your height or your net worth. That @$$ as you call him is more honest and authentic than you are because he is more aware of who he is than you are aware of who you are. That makes him appear more solid than you and women want solid even if it only appears to be solid.

The universe is a big mirror and you're a ghost. The universe cannot reflect a ghost, neater can a woman.

... Said Christian.

Jesus says:
You think 'dem boyz the baddies want aren't authentic? We'll, guess what? They are. They are more than you being Mr. people-pleasing nice-guy Christian.

... Said Christian.

Jesus says:

So they pretend and aren't as real as you, so what? You think they're not honest or authentic right?

Check this out Christian. They're reading a script, playing a role, doing their best to stay in character. They have picked a character in this game called life and that's that. They didn't pick the game or the rules. They abandoned their true self and left it way back there and lost it. They have come to truly believe that the character they are playing is who they are.

… Said Christian.

Jesus says:
You know Stanislavski? I am impressed Christian! This is The Method on the stage of life. Billions of people use this acting style every day and that is why Mr. Stanislavski had such a big impact. He simply described what we see all around us everyday. But not everyone is like that. You're not an actor or a character in a game or play and they're not like you Christian because you pick this game you chose these rules.

… Said Christian.

Jesus says:

You can pick the game, and the rules, or else you can be NPC.

... Said Christian.

Jesus says:

They are part of the game. They aren't playing the game.

We're all part of this game but, we're part of someone else's game and not our own - not in the beginning. The person playing the game in the beginning is God. We're born into this game as *Non-Player-Character* and if we remain as such our life is predestined based on the character we chose. After we choose a character, there aren't any other choices to be made. This is an easier way to live at first glance and life can look to be good or bad and it is all based on that choice. For some that choice largely where to go to college or weather or not to play sports as a kid. NPC parents tell their kids choices like this will make or break their future. That is only true if you are on something like an autopilot and not making choices day by day living a life indistinguishable from AI.

The real danger is not that computers will begin to think like man, but that

men will begin to think like computers
-Sydne J. Harris

… Said Christian.

I love to hear about your stories growing up and as a young man and it seems like you're starting to take control over your body and mind as a first-person player. It's your choice how far you go on this journey. You can pick a type or personality pre-programmed for us and live as the other NPCs do in this game and have a happy life. Or else you can choose every moment to be self aware and become your most authentic version of yourself. However if you choose this path you must embrace the Uberminch within or ask Yeshua to live in your heart which means the same thing. You will have to understand and embrace who you are. This is not a safe path Christian. This path has the highest stakes possible and you may find out who you are and not like it. You could lose your mind if you continue to ask questions and find answers about who you are and why you are here and where you were before this and where you will be after this.

… Said Christian.

Jesus says:

You think you can't be the most authentic version of yourself because of your background and the bullshit you went through?

… Said Christian.

Jesus says:

It sounds like your mother and father gave you plenty of opportunity and raised you in a nice house and you played sports. I don't see how bad things could have been.

… Said Christian.

Jesus says:

Didn't you go to private school your whole life and an expensive college? It seems like they spent plenty of money on you.

... Said Christian.

Jesus says:

I don't see how you could possibly be telling me this?

Your father sacrificed you?!

(sigh, I have seen this before)

It's pretty far out there, but I'm listening and believe it or not I know the feeling.

If you've got something to say, speak up! That kind of stuff used to happen a lot in the past, trust me I know, but you really think that happens today?

... Said Christian.

Jesus says:

You were sacrificed on Halloween??? **Moloch** you said???   Reeeeally... Now I'm really listening. (if you would like to know more about Moloch see From Harvard Divinity School *Author Russell Banks: Video: Feeding Moloch: The Sacrifice of Children on the Altar of Capitalism* *https://news-archive.hds.harvard.edu/news/2014/11/05feeding-moloch-sacrifice-children-altar-capitalism*

https://www.youtube.com/watch?v=Kv3Rbq5WIK4

… Said Christian.

Jesus says:

Maybe you should report this to the police or talk to a lawyer. Have you talked to the police about this?

… Said Christian.

Jesus says:
No way!

… Said Christian.

Jesus says:
Bahahahaha, the Supreme Court! And yes I know Suckerman Law in Washington DC. They provide protection for whistleblowers that provide information to the SEC and the IRS in the FTC and others. They are a special law firm and got their clients more reward money than you could believe thanks to Dodd-Frank legislation. That's wild! You did not shop your case at **DLA Piper, Gibson Dunn** and **Dorsey and Whitney**? You did? You did. Okay. So what did you do? What did they say?

… Said Christian.

Jesus says:
Unbelievable. You are a free man now. How did you break free? And what happened to Lu Ann?

Chapter 2

Articles Inc.

1918607

ARTICLES OF INCORPORATION OF
SPORTS ▮▮▮▮▮

A California Nonprofit Religious Corporation

FILED
In the office of the Secretary of State
of the State of California
DEC 16 1994
Tony Miller
Acting Secretary of State

One: The name of the corporation is SPORTS ▮▮▮▮▮

Two: This corporation is a religious corporation and is not organized for the private gain of any person. It is organized under the Nonprofit Religious Corporation Law primarily for religious purposes.

This corporation is organized and operated exclusively for religious purposes within the meaning of Section 501(c)(3) of the Internal Revenue Code of 1986 (or the corresponding section of any future United States internal revenue law). Notwithstanding any other provision of these articles, this corporation shall not, except to an insubstantial degree, engage in any activities or exercise any powers that are not in furtherance of the purposes of this corporation, and the corporation shall not carry on any other activities not permitted to be carried on (a) by a corporation exempt from federal income tax under Section 501(c)(3) of the Internal Revenue Code of 1986 or the corresponding provision of any future United States internal revenue law, or (b) by a corporation, contributions to which are deductible under Section 170(c)(2) of the Internal Revenue Code of 1986 or the corresponding provision of any future United States internal revenue law.

Three: The name and address in California of the corporation's initial agent for service of process are John N. Staples, III, Millard, Morris & Staples, Dolores and Sixth Streets, Carmel, CA 93921.

Four: (a) No substantial part of the activities of this corporation shall consist of carrying on propaganda, or otherwise attempting to influence legislation, and this corporation shall not participate in or intervene in (including publishing or distributing statements) any political campaign on behalf of any candidate for public office.

(b) The property of this corporation is irrevocably dedicated to religious purposes, as set forth in Article Two above. No part of the net earnings of this corporation shall inure to the benefit of its directors, trustees, officers, private shareholders or members, or to any individual.

(c) On the winding up and dissolution of this corporation, after paying or adequately providing for the debts and obligations of the corporation, the remaining assets of this corporation shall be distributed to an organization (or organizations) organized and operated exclusively for religious purposes and that is tax exempt under Section 501(c)(3) of the Internal Revenue Code of 1986.

Dated: December 15, 1994

_____
Kevin W. Fisher, Incorporator

I declare that I am the person who executed the above Articles of Incorporation, and that this instrument is my act and deed.

_____
Kevin W. Fisher, Incorporator

Articles of Incorporation of Sports Family Outreach
Page 2

NCTO

A0567238

1918607

**CERTIFICATE OF AMENDMENT
OF
ARTICLES OF INCORPATION**

FILED
In the office of the Secretary of State
of the State of California

JUN 0 8 2001

BILL JONES, Secretary of State

The undersigned certify that:

1. They are the **president** and the **secretary**, respectively, of Sports ███████ California corporation.

2. Article One of the Articles of Incorporation of this corporation is amended to read as follows: The name of the corporation is ███████ Sports ███████

3. The foregoing amendment of the Articles of Incorporation has been duly approved by the board of directors.

4. The corporation has no members.

We further declare under penalty of perjury under the laws of the State of California that the matters set forth in this certificate are true and correct of our own knowledge.

June 5, 2001

President

Secretary

Article VI: The period of duration of the corporation shall be perpetual.

Article VII: The personal liability of all of the directors of the corporation for monetary damages hereby eliminated to the fullest extent allowed as provided by the California Corporations Code, as the same may be supplemented and amended.

Article VIII: The corporation shall, to the fullest extent legally permissible under the provisions of the California Corporations Code, as the same may be amended and supplemented, shall indemnify and hold harmless any and all agents whom it shall have power to indemnify under said provisions from and against any and all liabilities (including expenses) imposed upon or reasonably incurred by him in connection with any action, suit or other proceeding in which he may be involved or with which he may be threatened, or other matters referred to in or covered by said provisions as to action in his official capacity, and shall continue as to a person who has ceased to be a director or officer of the corporation. Such indemnification shall not extend to those acts as specified by Section 204 (a)(10) of the California Corporations Code. Such indemnification provided shall not be deemed exclusive of any other rights to which those indemnified may be entitled under any Bylaw, Agreement or Resolution adopted by the shareholders entitled to vote thereon after notice.

Executed on this 30th day of July, 2004.

Zulma M. Howarth, Incorporator

ARTICLES OF INCORPORATION

OF

▬▬▬▬▬▬▬▬▬

The undersigned, a natural person, acting as an incorporator of a corporation under Title 1, Division 1, Chapter 2, California Corporations Code, adopt the following Articles of Incorporation of a business corporation:

Article I: The name of the corporation (hereinafter called the "corporation") is Sports Leadership Group

Article II: The purpose of the corporation is to engage in any lawful act or activity for which a corporation may be organized under the **GENERAL CORPORATION LAW** of California other than the banking business, the trust company business or the practice of a profession permitted to be incorporated by the California Corporations Code.

Article III: The name and address in the State of California of this corporation's initial agent for service of process is ▬▬▬▬▬▬, whose street address is 631 Silver Lake Drive,

Article IV: The total number of shares which the corporation shall have the authority to issue is one thousand (1,000), all of which are of a par value of one dollar ($1.00) each and classified as Common shares.

Article V: Shareholders shall be entitled as a matter of right to a preemptive right, for a period of thirty days, to subscribe for, purchase or receive any shares of the corporation which it may issue or sell, whether out of the number of shares authorized by these Articles of Incorporation or by amendment thereof, or out of the shares of the corporation acquired by it after the issuance thereof, any shareholder shall be entitled as a matter of right to purchase or subscribe for or receive any bonds, debentures, or other obligations which the corporation may issue or sell that shall be convertible into or exchangeable for shares, or to which shall be attached or shall appertain to any warrant or warrants or other instrument or instruments that shall confer upon the holder or owner of such obligation the right to subscribe for or purchase from the corporation any shares of any class or classes; and after the expiration of said thirty days, any and all of such shares, rights, bonds, debentures or other obligations which the corporation may issued, reissued, transferred, or granted by the Board of Directors, as the case may be, to such persons, firms, corporations, and associations, and for such lawful consideration, and on such terms, as the Board of Directors in its discretion may determine.

Chapter 3
A Return to Love:

"Our deepest fear is not that we are inadequate. Our deepest fear is that we are powerful beyond measure. It is our light, not our darkness that most frightens us. We ask ourselves, 'Who am I to be brilliant, gorgeous, talented, fabulous?' Actually, who are you not to be? You are a child of God. Your playing small does not serve the world. There is nothing enlightened about shrinking so that other people won't feel insecure around you. We are all meant to shine, as children do. We were born to make manifest the glory of God that is within us. It's not just in some of us; it's in everyone. And as we let our own light shine, we unconsciously give other people permission to do the same. As we are liberated from our own fear, our presence automatically liberates others."

— **Marianne Williamson, A Return to Love: Reflections on the Principles of "A Course in Miracles"**

Chapter 4

Listening to Jesus Podcast Podcast

This takes place at TheThirsTy3 ICEHOUSE

Jesus says

I like it here. It reminds me of that rough Bar where they bump into that Ranger smoking a pipe all by himself. *"Don't look too long at him though, he's a ranger and they are dangerous folk."* What do you get here?

… Said Christian.

Jesus says:

Indian Pale Ale it is! It comes in a pint??? I didn't know it would come in a pint. In a pint please, for me and my friends.

… Said Christian.

Jesus says:

She's beautiful. I see what you mean about her presence and, how did you say it; I never heard someone say it quite like that.

Jesus says:

Well said, so it's not because she treats you special but it's because she treats everyone special that you're so attracted to her, because you know that you're a special person with high privilege that a lot of people would want to impress so treating you special means little to nothing. Treating everyone special that means that she's special! Whereas if she treats just you special that means that just you are special.

Jesus says:

So have you asked her out or told her how you feel?

Jesus says:

Is it you or her that's distracted with ADHD, and occasionally drunk? You got to speak plainly and directly. I know you say you do but clearly you don't. Why don't you try writing it down so you can see exactly trying to say. pretend she's sitting right in front of you and you're right her later or you talking to her. That way you can go back and reread it to try to understand what the heck you're talking about because your ENERGY your POWER is scattered.

Jesus says:

Christian you don't have to explain yourself. I just don't know why you're still talking about it. You spent that money your father and mother gave you. You made an investment in *Eye-On America Energy Corporation* and it failed. Get over it. You need to take responsibility for your own actions. Like what we were talking about last week about the NPCs all among us. You're sounding like one. And not a cool bad boy that gets all the ladies you sound like whiny ungrateful spoiled kid of a legacy of first person players. You can be a complainer soggy and sad if you want but I don't understand that. You're better than that. I don't know them that well but maybe your pastor, your father and your trustee are too. And I don't know for a fact, but maybe Mr. J is better than that too.

Jesus says:

I know your Big Papa very well. He is a legend! One of the founders of PRO-Football and helped **The Artist** (Prince) with his night club in St.Paul... Bob Dylan and THE STONES with that thing.

Jesus says:

He helped a US Senator or two out with that other thing... you know.

... Said Christian.

No, not that thing. That other thing. It's no big deal. Fugetabout-it.

... Said Christian.

-Jesus says

You don't have to tell me. I know Jack Kemp and Jesse Ventura. Goddamn! I know about Father and Pastor and your Trustee too but I never meet them; I just don't know these men. Either way, his career and life is legendary too and I read all about him in the sports papers. They were the original ones to take a knee for a cause in PRO-Football along with Mr. J. And Mr. D gave them his full support. These aren't bad men, they can't be.

... Said Christian.

Jesus says:
You don't seem disabled.

... Said Christian.

Jesus says

You're being dramatic. Free POWER? How could something like that go unnoticed?

... Said Christian.

Jesus says:

So the story goes, EyeOn America Energy servers were secretly installed in the underground parking garage at the Googleplex in Mountain View and at Amazon and that's how they got so big over the last 20 years with a free ENERGY, FREE POWER, machine. That's quite the story. But sounds a little too obviously *conspiracy theory illuminati* to actually be the hidden hand of these massive tech companies to get free POWER. Plus why would they let you invest?

... Said Christian.

Jesus says:

Oh right I forgot about your high Privilege you were born into. Right on.

Said Christian.

Jesus says:

I get that but c'mon Her Majesty the Queen in her right of Alberta, the Crown Prince next in line to rule The Kingdom through the Vision Fund, the wealthiest man in Japan, and N.M. Rothschild and sons, the wealthiest American family, the Waltons? Madrone Capital? That is quite the list of people to co-invest with.

https://www.bloomberg.com/news/articles/2023-08-06/saudi-wealth-fund-takes-15-6-billion-hit-from-softbank-and-tech

... Said Christian.

Jesus says:

Christian you have for the best stories man. Cheers to you and the Magna Carta you love so much. This document is the basis for common law that trust law is built upon. This allowed us to keep a king in line and paved the way for The French Revolution and The American Revolution. I could talk about property rights and trust law for days but so could you.

... Said Christian.

Jesus says:
Yes trust and common law form our society and if it started there so be it. But you weren't a slave c'mon man nobody was making you do anything. I'm sorry you felt like your money and name had been stolen and used for the financial gain of these men.

... Said Christian.

You're standing in twilight Christian. C'mon and join me in the light. It feels so good to be yourself and I promise the ladies are going to love you for it.

It's just like what we were talking about on the podcast last week about nonplayer characters and first person characters. You are powerful beyond measure if you decide to play your own character instead of using autopilot all the time which is programmed by all the big marketing and advertising companies.

It's like it's your light not your darkness that frightens you. Have you ever hear that quote?

"Hi, my name's Lu Ann and I'm a first person player."

Five minutes ago She sat down next to Jesus at the bar there at TheThirsTy3 ICEHOUSE she had to say hi. This is how Jesus met Lu Ann.

... Said Christian.

Jesus says:
You heard that quote at your high school football chapel before a game that's amazing.

We heard this song before the Big Game against San Diego.

Things Are Gonna Change

Song by Bryan Duncan

This song got me through some of the roughest times of my life because sometimes I don't sleep at knight but you know what? Things are gonna change.

Chapter 5

Psychological evaluation

PSYCHOLOGICAL EVALUATION

1024 El Capitan
Danville, CA 94526

Date: 1/3/03
Parents:
Birthdate: 10/5/84

BACKGROUND

At the present time ▓▓▓ is a senior in high school, anticipating entry as a college freshman in the Fall of 2003. I have evaluated ▓▓▓ several times since 1994, and have tracked his academic progress and his academic difficulties over a period of nine years.

▓▓▓ is a well-adjusted adolescent with a range of interests highlighted by athletics. He has played football competitively, including high school varsity football. ▓▓▓ has strived for academic achievement. Because of his reading delays, he has had to work hard, and has applied himself diligently over the years of his schooling. ▓▓▓ has a history of reading problems, for which he has received special services through the pubic schools. He has also received private remedial instruction.

In 1997 ▓▓▓ was in a bicycle accident in which he sustained serious injuries, including a concussion and facial injury. I conducted evaluative assessments of ▓▓▓ in June and July of 2001, between April and June of 1999, and in February of 1994. As well, the San Ramon Valley Unified School District conducted assessments in 1999 and in 1996.

Across a range of assessments over nearly a decade and with different examiners ▮▮▮ has consistently demonstrated a pattern of high intelligence and low reading and writing scores. He exemplifies a bright student with a classic learning disability in symbol-processing, visual and visual-motor processing that have resulted in academic delays in reading and writing.

COGNITIVE, INTELLECTUAL, ACADEMIC, AND NEUROPSYCHOLOGICAL FUNCTIONING

Ability

In 2001, assessment measures portrayed ▮▮▮ intellectual functioning overall in the average range of intelligence, with verbal ability in the high-average range and nonverbal ability in the average range. His scores on the Wechsler Intelligence Scale for Children-III (WISC-III) were: Full Scale IQ=▮▮ Verbal IQ=▮▮ Performance IQ=▮▮ Verbal Comprehension Index (verbal scores factored without the Arithmetic subtest) was ▮▮ His Perceptual Organization Index was ▮▮ and his Freedom from Distractibility Index was ▮▮ It should be noted that the average range is from ▮▮

▮▮▮ has historically demonstrated a discrepancy between Verbal and Performance IQs, showing significantly higher verbal skills. In 1999, his Wechsler Intelligence Scale for Children-III (WISC-III) scores were: Full Scale IQ=▮▮ Verbal IQ=▮▮ Performance IQ=▮▮

In 1994, his Wechsler Intelligence Scale for Children-III (WISC-III) scores were: Full Scale IQ=▮▮ Verbal IQ=▮▮ Performance IQ=▮▮ The degree of this decline in overall scores is unexpected, and would not be predicted by either statistical regression or developmental averaging as ▮▮▮ matured between the ages of 10 and 16 years. A 9-

point standard score drop in verbal skills is unlikely. Moreover, the greater decline in both verbal and nonverbal scores occurred between 1994 and 1999. █████ suffered the bicycle accident in 1997.

████ demonstrated a cognitive style that favors assimilation of knowledge through language, symbolic and semantic meaning, and verbal concepts. People with ████ pattern of strengths (verbal fluency, conceptual reasoning, vocabulary, general knowledge fund) and weaknesses (visual thinking, attention to detail, visual-motor speed and accuracy) tend to learn better through talking and exchanging verbal information and ideas than through nonverbal (i.e ████████████████████ methods. They also tend to be more efficient at describing than doing ██

On the 2001 examination, he obtained a Coding standard score=6 (compared with 5 in 1999) and a Mazes standard score=11 (compared with 7 in 1999).

While the Coding score is a low score corresponding to his performance on this measure previously ████ performance o ████ mproved significantly, reflecting much improved abilities at planning and visual organization.

attention

████ attentional processes were assessed via multiple measures. These included specific subtest scores, test comparisons, factor analysis, electroencephalography, interviews and reports, questionnaires, and clinical observations. One reliable measure employed was the Test of Variables of Attention (TOVA). The TOVA (Test of Variables of Attention) is a computerized assessment of central nervous system response; it is quite effective in detecting performances which are associated with attentional deficits and other deviations in nervous system functioning. The TOVA is a continuous performance test that measures four variables: Inattention, Impulsivity, Response Time, and Variability.

Two important points should be mentioned about the TOVA. First, this continuous performance test requires the examinee to maintain attention to a simple task for a period of time without interacting with others. Daydreaming, attention-seeking, and attempts to "take a break" are all factored into the results. Thus, the test reflects cortical self-regulation and central nervous system problems, and provides important information about independent task accomplishment, adaptation without social or interpersonal cues, and attempts to manipulate a demand situation.

Second, TOVA scores are extremely sensitive to slight performance deviations -- this is what makes the test so diagnostically useful. Thus, although the scores are rendered in standardized Gaussian distribution numbers, the extremity of the deviation scores must be interpreted with caution, especially in comparison with traditional range of ability or achievement levels.

The current TOVA administration yielded a statistically invalid protocol. This was due to the high rate of anticipatory error ▓▓▓ committed. Anticipatory errors occur when the subject responds too quickly, even before the computer flashes the stimulus. It represents a form of impulsive neurosynaptic perseveration, in which the nervous system gets overstimulated and cannot properly self-regulate and adjust its timing. Because of the statistical invalidity, it is not appropriate to report standard scores from this TOVA.

Another indication of attentional difficulties is the WISC-III Freedom from Distractibility Index. ▓▓▓ score of ▓▓ though clearly in the average range, was significantly lower than his verbal ability scores.

With regard to attentional and executive control functions, exhibited numerous subtle signs of a disregulated nervous system which are often present in attention deficit disorders. This central nervous system pattern affects academic symbolic tasks as well as follow-through and organizational behaviors. Disinhibition and erratic regulation of perception and arousal make task-specific reading into stressful work.

Supplementing the neuropsychological performance measures, a clinical encephalogram and quantitative EEG analysis (QEEG) were conducted. These results were analyzed and interpreted by a neurologist (Meyer Proler, M.D.) and another neuropsychologist (Jack Johnstone, Ph.D.).

The general interpretation of ▮▮▮ EEG and QEEG is as follows: The conventional medical EEG was within normal limits for his age group. The QEEG contained some increased slow activity, but was generally within normal limits for his age.

The slowing of the EEG that would be considered abnormal was especially apparent over the frontotemporal regions, occurring during reading and math tasks. There was also a sporadic excess of delta and theta activity in the left hemisphere and poor interhemispheric coherence values in the occipital region. Increased theta-beta ratios were observed at ▮▮▮ sites.

The general picture is one of a brain that is disease-free, but has some focal slowing, particularly in the brain regions associated with ▮▮▮▮▮▮▮▮▮ This pattern is quite consistent with learning disorders and with attention deficit syndromes characterized by disinhibition and poor maintenance of focused and divided attention.

Overall, the current EEG and QEEG are better than the ones from 1999. The slowing patterns of EEG are often seen in head injury, and can also be characteristic of regressed or immature neurological function of diverse etiology. The minimal amount of hypocoherence suggests a poor integration of left- and right-brain functions and a slight but persistent cortical disorganization.

People with systemic vulnerabilities often respond to the trauma of head injury by perseverating and maintaining inefficient and disregulated brain patterns long after the injury. Possibly minor pre-morbid tendencies potentiate into extended and more rigidified patterns after head trauma. This would appear to be the case with ▮▮▮ where his predisposition to learning difficulties and disregulation was greatly impacted by the head trauma. The adverse net effect is that the brain is pre-occupied with healing and recovery of function at the expense of reduction in pace and quality of processing and the learning of new material. That has been able to recover from his injury and continue with his academic achievement despite both developmental and environmental adversity) is testimony to his ability and potential to succeed academically.

neuropsychological functioning, memory, and modality processing

███████ performance on the Wide Range Assessment of Memory and Learning was deficient. He earned a Memory Screening Index ████ (standard score), corresponding to the 12 percentile.

On the Wide Range Assessment of ███████████████████████████ 16 percentile ███ ██ His score on the █████ ██ 1 percentile. This task requires ████████████████████████████ He scored in the average range (50 percentile) on Verbal Learning, a repetitive list-learning test, and Story Memory, which uses a narrative format requiring sequencing and integration.

This pattern is excessively variable (3.0 standard deviations), and it is consistent with a pattern of learning disabilities. The lower scores on ████████████████████████ ██ higher scores on Verbal Learning, and Story Memory reflect ████████ stronger and preferred modalities of auditory and verbal learning.

visual, visuo-spatial, & visual-motor processing

███████ was assessed on measures of visual processing, visuo-spatial thinking, visual-motor speed and integration, and mental "mapping" of problem-solving.

From previous testing, his Wechsler Performance Scale pattern suggests weaknesses in right cerebral cognition and in planning and execution of pencil-and-paper tasks. On the

Wechsler Intelligence Scale for Children-III administered in 1994, ▉ scored at the 63 percentile (standard score=11) on Coding, a measure of visual-motor speed and clerical efficiency. In 1999, he scored at the 5 percentile (standard score=5). This time around, he scored at the 9 percentile (standard score=6). On the 1994 administration of Mazes, ▉ scored at the 2 percentile (standard score=4). In 1999, he scored at the 16 percentile (standard score=7). In 2001, he scored at the 63 percentile (standard score=11).

People who perform as ▉ did on these tests commonly struggle with copying, note-taking, and sifting information from the environment into cogent written form. They typically do not like, and do not perform paperwork well. The practical evidence of this shows in ▉ poor writing and spelling. There is a neuropsychological processing problem that results in dysfunction in this domain.

Comprehensive assessment of cerebral integrity and modality preference and efficiency includes measurement of problem-solving through tactile-kinesthetic learning and memory. In this regard, one performance series from the Halstead-Reitan Neuropsychological Battery is particularly noteworthy: the Tactual Performance Test. This test is a measure of complex psychomotor ability that includes a strong problem-solving component. On this task, the examinee, while blindfolded, is required to place variously shaped blocks in their proper places on a formboard. The first trial is done with the preferred hand, the second trial with the non-preferred hand, and the third trial with both hands. Neurologically, this test provides information concerning the integrated functions of tactile, proprioceptive, and kinesthetic input with the efficiency of motor performance. The Tactual Performance Test requires skills from each cerebral hemisphere and provides a comparison of the efficiency of performance as an indication of the biological adequacy of each cerebral hemisphere. Psychologically, the Tactual Performance Test provides considerable information concerning a person's ability to use his hands in a problem-solving situation.  performance on this series scored in the normal range for time and memory, but in the mildly impaired range for localization. These results correlate highly with adequacy in problem-solving through spatial,

proprioceptive, and tactile cues. His performance indicates a mild impairment in the
██████████████████████████████████████
████████████████████

In comparison with the 1999 Tactual Performance Test ████ improved in memory, but got worse in localization. This represents an improved sensory registration and probable hemispheric integration, but a continuing impairment in the ability to properly encode and utilize spatial information. These data predict that ████ will have difficulty in the apprehension of visual and nonverbal stimuli ██████████████████████████
██
██████████████████████████

abstraction, reasoning, & logical analysis

Effective learning and adaptive functioning depend upon properly developed abstraction and reasoning abilities, conceptual thinking, and logical analysis. Although these abilities are fundamental to intelligence, they are often inadequately measured by tests with high saturation of content and acquired facts. To assess these more basic abilities, the Category Test (from the Halstead-Reitan Neuropsychological Battery) was administered. This test is very sensitive to brain impairment, and it measures the ability of a person to reason with adequate cause-and-effect thinking and to use both positive and negative experiences to alter performance. It also reflects impairments in judgment often shown by those with attentional and other neuropsychological deficiencies. Although the Category Test is not particularly difficult for most normal people, it is a relatively complex concept formation test that requires ability to (1) note recurring similarities and differences in stimulus material; (2) postulate reasonable hypotheses about these similarities and differences; (3) test these hypotheses by receiving positive or negative reinforcement (bell or buzzer); and (4) adapt hypotheses based on the reinforcement following each response. The Category Test requires the examinee to use abstraction to postulate possible solutions in a structured (rather than permissive) context. On this test,

▇▇▇ score of 26 errors fell within the normal range. Interpretively, it appears that he does use adequate reasoning, abstraction, and information from his own experiences to determine meaningful relationships among events.

Other measures from the Halstead-Reitan Neuropsychological Battery were administered to comprehensively evaluate ▇▇▇ mental flexibility, reasoning faculties, organizational and expressive skills. ▇▇▇ performed *inadequately* on both Trail Making A and Trail Making B (from the Halstead-Reitan Neuropsychological Battery). These are visual-motor based tests that require immediate recognition of the symbolic significance of numbers and letters, the ability to scan the page continuously to identify the next letter or number in sequence, flexibility in integrating the numerical and alphabetic series, and completion of these requirements under the pressure of time. These tests differ in that Trail Making A requires linear sequential performance, and Trail Making B requires the combination of visual-spatial fluidity and the mental flexibility to change set when executing a timed visual-motor task. Adequate performance on these tests reflects the brain's ability to distinguish relevant attributes and differences in a demand situation and, therefore, provides vital predictive information about the person's ability to adapt flexibly to changing circumstances and demands. Inadequate performances on these tests correlate with difficulties in making transitions, pacing, planning, remaining on track, and achieving fluid success with printed or written material. ▇▇▇ performance on Trail Making A ranked within the impaired range and Trail Making B ranked within the mildly impaired range.

This slow speed in processing visually-based symbolic information is a handicap. ▇▇▇▇▇▇▇▇▇▇▇▇▇▇▇▇▇▇▇▇▇▇▇▇▇▇▇▇▇▇▇▇

academic achievement

▇▇▇ achievement test profile showed performances ranging from average to deficient. On the Wide Range Achievement Test-3, he earned the following standard scores: Reading ▇▇ (fifth grade level), Spelling ▇▇ (sixth grade level), Arithmetic ▇▇ (seventh grade level).

These scores (virtually equivalent to his 1999 scores), signify low achievement —
significantly below the levels predicted by his intellect. For example, a person with an IQ
of 100 would be expected to improve one grade level in content achievement per year. A
person with a verbal IQ one standard deviation higher than 100 (such as ▓▓▓ would
be expected to make more than a year's academic growth in one year. However, ▓▓▓
Wide Range Achievement Test-3 Reading score in 1999 was at the fourth grade level and
his current score was at the fifth grade level. His 1999 Spelling score was at the fifth
grade level and his current Spelling score was at the sixth grade level. His Arithmetic
score was at the seventh grade level both in 1999 and in 2001.

On other, more comprehensive tests, ▓▓▓ fared worse. On the Gray Oral Reading
Test-3, ▓▓▓ earned a standard score of ▓▓ with grade level equivalencies ranging from
second to fourth. The Gray Oral Reading Test-3 is a more realistic measure of reading
than other tests, because it requires actual reading of passages under timed conditions,
along with choosing the right answers to comprehension questions. ▓▓▓
performance indicates enormous difficulty with reading fluency. In 1999, he scored a
standard score of ▓▓ on this test.

On the Nelson-Denny, a silent reading test ▓▓▓ earned the following scores:
Vocabulary=▓▓ (16 percentile); Comprehension=▓▓ (3 percentile); Total test ▓▓ (4
percentile); Reading Rate=1 percentile.

On the Test of Written Language-3 ▓▓▓ earned a standard score of ▓▓ (13 percentile).
This compares less favorably with his 1999 score of ▓▓ and reflects his difficulties with
encoding as well as decoding print. This is a student who concurrently scored at the 95
percentile on an intellectual measure of verbal reasoning and at the 75 percentile in
vocabulary

Thus, evaluative assessments across time and multiple specific tests have consistently
reflected significant discrepancies between ▓▓▓ intelligence and his academic

achievement. In the most recent assessment (2001), these discrepancies reached as much as 47 standard score points (between Wechsler Verbal IQ and the Gray Oral Reading Test-3) and consistently exceeded 20 standard score points across measures when compared with the most stringent and conservative criteria.

SUMMARY AND RECOMMENDATIONS

███ has a history of reading problems, for which he has received special services through the pubic schools. He has also received private remedial instruction. I conducted evaluative assessments of ███ in June and July of 2001, between April and June of 1999, and in February of 1994. As well, the San Ramon Valley Unified School District conducted assessments in 1999 and in 1996.

In 1997 ███ was in a bicycle accident in which he sustained serious injuries, including a concussion and facial injury. Though some of the erratic fluctuations in test scores may reflect the effects of head injury, ███ has recovered sufficiently to pursue higher education. However, he will need accommodations to assist him in achieving up to his potential.

In 2001, assessment measures portrayed ███'s intellectual functioning overall in the average range of intelligence, with verbal ability in the high-average range and nonverbal ability in the average range. His scores on the Wechsler Intelligence Scale for Children-███ Verbal Comprehension Index (verbal scores factored without the Arithmetic subtest) was ███ His Perceptual Organization Index was ███ and his Freedom from Distractibility Index was ███ It should be noted that the average range is from ███

███ has historically demonstrated a discrepancy between Verbal and Performance IQs, showing significantly higher verbal skills. In 1999, his Wechsler Intelligence Scale for Children-III (WISC-III) scores were: Full Scale IQ=███ Verbal IQ=███ Performance

IQ=94.

The 2001 neuropsychological examination revealed evidence of mild attention deficit and central nervous system disregulation.

The general interpretation of ▓▓▓ EEG and QEEG is as follows: The conventional medical EEG was within normal limits for his age group. The QEEG contained some increased slow activity, but was generally within normal limits for his age.

The slowing of the EEG that would be considered abnormal was especially apparent over the frontotemporal regions, occurring during reading and math tasks. There was also a sporadic excess of delta and theta activity in the left hemisphere and poor interhemispheric coherence values in the occipital region and elevated theta-beta ratios over left parietal and midline sites.

The general picture is one of a brain that is disease-free, but has some focal slowing, particularly in the brain regions associated with cognitive processing of print and symbols. This pattern is quite consistent with learning disorders and with attention deficit syndromes characterized by disinhibition and poor maintenance of focused and divided attention.

People with systemic vulnerabilities often respond to the trauma of head injury by perseverating and maintaining inefficient and disregulated brain patterns long after the injury. Possibly minor pre-morbid tendencies potentiate into extended and more rigidified patterns after head trauma. This would appear to be the case with ▓▓▓ where his predisposition to learning difficulties and disregulation was greatly impacted by the head trauma. The adverse net effect is that the brain is pre-occupied with healing and recovery of function at the expense of reduction in pace and quality of processing and the learning of new material. That ▓▓▓ has been able to recover from his injury and continue with his academic achievement (despite both developmental and environmental adversity) is testimony to his ability and potential to succeed academically.

With regard to emotional and psychological development, ▇▇▇ appeared well-adjusted. His MMPI and Rorschach protocols indicate a well-adjusted adolescent. Given his history of difficulties and trauma, this adjustment is remarkable. He has great strengths of character, including persistence, a hard-working nature, and a compassionate heart for people.

Evaluative assessments across time and multiple specific tests have consistently reflected significant discrepancies between ▇▇▇ intelligence and his academic achievement. In the most recent assessment (2001), these discrepancies reached as much as 47 standard score points (between Wechsler Verbal IQ and the Gray Oral Reading Test-3) and consistently exceeded 20 standard score points across measures when compared with the most stringent and conservative criteria.

These data predict that ▇▇▇ will have difficulty in the apprehension of visual and nonverbal stimuli (necessary to picture, sequence, or construct outcomes, as well as to understand how things fit together). These cognitive skills are critical to appreciating the symbolic significance of encoded material (such as test questions), and the inferential comprehension of unstated themes.

statement of disability

▇▇▇ disability is a cognitive processing disorder that affects his attention, distractibility, speed of processing and writing information, and reading. His neuropsychological processing irregularities interfere with efficient symbol-processing and synthesis of visual integration. His learning disability impedes his ability to process information and express his responses under time pressure. He requires significantly longer amounts of time to process and respond to visual data, both serial and simultaneous, than do most individuals. This affects his ability to assimilate (especially visual) information, and to organize and express his thoughts under time constraints. He will tend to underrepresent his knowledge in a timed testing situation, particularly one in which he does not have access to proofreading and spellchecking tools. His processing style includes the need for more time to write down thoughts and to double-check and proofread material. ███ requirement for time and attention to these mechanics exceeds that of his peers.

In addition ███ has a significant reading disability which affects his fluency and comprehension.

This condition has existed since at least 1994, and is not the result of environmental deprivation, motivational variables, or emotional disturbance.

In the measurement of his performance, however, ███ s penalized by paper-and-pencil tests which require intensive scanning of visual symbols, including the organization and proofreading of ideas in handwritten form. It simply takes him longer to wade through the visual array. The printed items force him to picture in his mind (without the aid of reference or computing tools) the sequential relationships that he is so adept at doing verbally. These efforts take him more time and algorithms which, in turn, increase his fatigue and anxiety, thus negatively impacting test performance. The nonverbal testing situation disadvantages ███ because it artificially separates the verbal and nonverbal processing of information. Although this is not problematic for many people, such testing underestimates the knowledge and capabilities of those with specific learning disabilities. It is, therefore, necessary and appropriate to accommodate ███ learning differences. He needs special adaptations in the assessment of his skills in order to properly reflect his competence.

███ will require the following accommodations:

1. He should be allowed extra time on exams, at least double the length of time traditionally allotted.

2. Lengthy exams should be divided into segments of testing in order to relieve the strain imposed by having to endure prolonged periods of expressing his knowledge

through media that adversely impact his learning disability.

3. ████ should be allowed to use a computer/word processor when taking exams requiring written composition. The recommended accommodations would not fundamentally alter the measurement of skills and knowledge the exams are intended to test.

4. Where possible, ████ should be given the opportunity to take oral tests.

5. ████ should be allowed to tape record lectures and other class material.

6. ████ should have access to professors for individual meetings throughout each semester.

7. ████ should have access to a college-based learning assistance center with services including reading review and interpretation, test-taking strategies, intermediary communications with professors, and academic counseling.

[signature]
_____

Mark Steinberg, Ph.D.

Licensed Psychologist
Licensed Educational Psychologist
Clinical Neuropsychologist

Chapter 6

The Perfect Storm: NPD & BPD

HillBilly Elegy A Memoir of a Family and Culture in Crisis is a bestselling 2016

memoir by J. D. Vance

Hillbilly Elegy: Directed by Ron Howard. With Amy Adams, Glenn Close, Gabriel Basso, Haley Bennett.

More about this in the second edition.

All families and people have problems and struggles.

This Chapter is left blank intentionally.

Chapter 7

Listening to Jesus Podcast

Christian arrives to the studio early to meet with Jesus

Jesus says:

Cm'on in Christian! I was just listening to Phil Collins In the Air Tonight

... Said Christian.

Jesus says:

You've been through a lot Christian and I can tell the betrayal you felt was hard to bear. I think you've handled it very well, given the circumstances you were thrown into.

... Said Christian.

Jesus says:

I'm starting to understand now the money you got from the incident that happened on Halloween you never really got did you?

You really believe that money was spent sending you to Waco and it felt was a a death sentence? You think child sacrifice should be illegal. It is sir. It is.

... Said Christian.

Jesus says:

I'm glad you took me up on the writing challenge every day and I am using the journal I gave you. I understand you communicate through an Attorney when it comes to father and mother and of corse your former Trustee who you couldn't TRUST. What about Mr. J.? Have you thought about writing him a personal letter? You could use the journal I gave you. Maybe he didn't mean any harm doesn't sound like it and it sounds like you weren't the only one duped AND led to losses by EyeOn America Energy Corporation. What you're saying is true, you're in good company because they also fooled the wealthiest and most powerful royal families, companies, and people in the world. You walk and talk like you're one of them and I guess I understand.

This thing of ours as you say -

You were born into this thing and you're going to be a part of it for life and there's nothing that will change that.

... Said Christian.

Jesus says:

Look, I was born into some privilege as well but the difference is I don't have to talk about it. I know you trust me and this is for the podcast otherwise you wouldn't... but I understand you don't wanna talk about this anymore.

... Said Christian.

Jesus says.

Yeah, that's how the story goes that Yeshua loved that woman more than anyone and maybe she was a dirty slut.... But who cares, she loves passionately and deeply, and cared for Yeshua, in a special way. He didn't need some...

... Said Christian.

Jesus says

Oh shit, Lu Ann. So did you lock it down with her or not?

... Said Christin.

Jesus says:

So you wrote down everything you wanted to tell her and you gave her it all in a letter?

Said Christian.

Jesus says:

A whole notebook of letters? Are you crazy guy? You are a sick guy, you know that I didn't tell you to do all that? Just kidding, yes I did! I'm glad you did it even though she may not get it. It's not about her, it's about you brother. I know that wasn't easy and you got a very high chance of rejection here, but you know what fuck it! You do you.

Said Christian.

Jesus says:

I'm glad you can appreciate her for that hybrid creature she is I realize you can appreciate her just for the way she is and likewise appreciate yourself a little bit more because I promise you the good you see in her is good that is in you no matter how far down it is. It's in there somewhere. I also understand it's hard sometimes when you've been betrayed by the people Who are supposed to love you and care for you like your family and starting over you don't wanna let anyone in but someone's gonna slip through the cracks you're gonna love someone. You're going to see the good in someone if you're lucky and you're gonna pull through.

This podcast concludes with playing In The Air Tonight by Phil Collins

Chapter 8

Hedge Fund Gate Capital

■■■ Partners, A Delaware Multiple Series LLC

Summary of Individual Partner Capital Account

March 31, 2015

Opening Capital, 12/31/14	■■■
Contributions	-
Other Income / (Expenses)	(1)
Realized Gains / (Losses)	-
Unrealized Gains / (Losses)	-
Distributions	-
Ending Capital, 3/31/15	■■■

Company	Cost	Fair Value
■■■ Energy Corporation	■■■	■■■
■■■ Energy Corporation	■■■	■■■
■■■ Energy Corporation	■■■	■■■
■■■ Energy Corporation	■■■	■■■
Total Investments	■■■	
Other assets / liabilities, net	■■■	
Total Net Assets	■■■	

This Page Shows The TOTAL Investments by ■■■ / or on his behalf.

COMPANY'S SIGNATURE PAGE

ACCEPTING MEMBER: ███████

INVESTMENT OPPORTUNITY ███████ A Delaware Multiple Series LLC ███████

CLOSING TIME:

    MONTH: March
    DAY: 6
    YEAR: 2006
    TIME: 5:00 P.M.

Effective as of the Closing Time:

1. The Company hereby acknowledges and accepts the Notice of Acceptance of the Accepting Member to invest in the Investment Opportunity, and, if such Accepting Member has not been previously admitted to the Company, hereby admits the Accepting Member to the Company as a Non-Managing Member.

2. The Accepting Member's Series Capital Commitment with respect to the Investment Opportunity is hereby deemed to equ███████ which amount shall be set forth as the Accepting Member's Series Capital Commitment on Schedule A to the Operating Agreement.

Executed this 6th day of March, 2006.

███████ PARTNERS,
a Delaware Multiple Series LLC

By: ███████

Name: ███████
Title: Managing Member

███████ PARTNERS,
A DELAWARE MULTIPLE SERIES LLC

NOTICE OF ACCEPTANCE OF AN INVESTMENT OPPORTUNITY IN

███████ A Delaware Multiple Series LLC ███████

ACCEPTING MEMBER:

███████
Name

Please complete the information below:

Full Legal Name of Accepting Member: ███████
Contact Person: ███████
Address: 631 Silver Lake Dr.
City, State and Zip: ███████
E-mail Address: ███████
Telephone Number: ███████
Fax Number: _____

Accepting Member's State/Nation of Domicile (for individuals) or
Principal Place of Business (for entities): CALIFORNIA/USA
Accepting Member's Social Security or Tax Identification Number: ███████

Accredited Investor Questionnaire

Please check all that apply of the following:

(1) [X] I am a natural person whose net worth, either individually or jointly with my spouse, now exceeds $1,000,000.

(2) [ ] I am a natural person whose individual income was in excess of $200,000, or whose joint income with my spouse was in excess of $300,000, in each of the last two calendar years, and I reasonably expect to reach the same income level in the current calendar year.

(3) [ ] I am a corporation, trust or partnership that (i) has total assets in excess of $5,000,000; and (ii) was not organized or reorganized for the specific purpose of acquiring securities of the Company.

(4) [ ] I am an investment company registered under the Investment Company Act of 1940 or a business development company as defined in Section 2(a)(48) of the Investment Company Act.

Chapter 9

Marcus Aurelius Meditations

...ourselves be distracted. That is not allowed. Instead, as if you were dying right now, despise your flesh. A mess of blood, pieces of bone, a woven tangle of nerves, veins, arteries. Consider what the spirit is: air, and never the same air, but vomited out and gulped in again every instant. Finally, the intelligence. Think of it this way: You are an old man. Stop allowing your mind to be a slave, to be jerked about by selfish impulses, to kick against fate and the present, and to mistrust the future.

[2.3] What is divine is full of Providence. Even chance is not divorced from nature, from the interweaving and enfolding of things governed by Providence. Everything proceeds from it. And then there is necessity and the needs of the whole world, of which you are a part. Whatever the nature of the whole does, and whatever serves it to maintain it, is good for every part of nature. The world is maintained by change – in the elements and in the things they compose. That should be enough for you; treat it as an axiom. Discard your thirst for books, so that you won't die in bitterness, but in cheerfulness and truth, grateful to the gods from the bottom of your heart.

[2.4] Remember how long you've been putting this off, how many extensions the gods gave you, and you didn't use them. At some point you have to recognize what the world it is that you belong to; what power rules it and from what source you spring; that there is a limit to the time assigned you, and if you don't use it to free yourself it will be gone and will never return.

[2.5] Concentrate every minute like a Roman – like a man - on doing what's in front of you with precise and genuine seriousness, tenderly, willingly, with justice. And on freeing yourself from all other distractions. Yes, you can – if you do everything as if it were the last thing you were doing in your life, and stop being aimless, stop letting your emotions override what your mind tells you, stop being hypocritical, self-centered, irritable. You see how few things you have to do to live a satisfying and reverent life? If you can manage this, that's all even the gods can ask of you. [2.6] Yes, keep on degrading yourself, soul. But soon your chance at dignity will be gone. Everyone gets one life. Yours is almost used up, and instead of treating yourself with respect, you have entrusted your own happiness to the souls of others.

[2.7] Do external things distract you? Then make time for yourself to learn something worthwhile; stop letting yourself be pulled in all directions. But make sure you guard against the other kind of confusion. People who labor all their lives but have no purpose to direct every thought and impulse toward are wasting their time — even when hard at work. [2.8] Ignoring what goes on in other people's souls – no one ever came to grief that way. But if you won't keep track of what your own soul's doing, how can you not be unhappy? [2.9] Don't ever forget these things:

The nature of the world

My nature.

How I relate to the world.

What proportion of it I make up.

That you are a part of nature, and no one can prevent you from speaking and acting in harmony with it, always.

Marcus Aurelius – Excerpts – page 2

[4.4] If thought is something we share, than so is reason – what makes up reasoning beings. If so, then the reason that tells us what to do and what not to do is also shared. And if so, we share a common law.

Chapter 10

Jesus' Mirror Athena

Some people believe that Yeshua in the Bible is a symbol for your best self. 100% present in this moment. Fully man and fully God. A symbol for who you are when you are present and authentic. Some people believe God the father is your past before you became present. God moved on earth until Yeshua came to earth then it was his turn. Then Yeshua had to leave for the spirit to move on the earth. Some people believe…

Christian has realized he has to perfect himself in his own internal universe, because if he doesn't do that he can't perfect and contribute to his eternal universe. I specifically mean when it comes to his **Petition to End the Human Races.** *Every action has an equal and opposite reaction,* we cannot just work to help one group of people. We must work to help all groups of people at the same time simultaneously otherwise it's not gonna go so well or as well as it could. Minority groups have difficult times, but everyone is a minority of some group. No group faces more discrimination than people with disabilities according to USA.GOV

Christian is born into a privileged family that is high privilege because of their, I don't know religious standing or inherited power. His family was also abusive. His parents would tell a story to the members of their church about their small child getting out of bed and they would politely say, go back to bed. This would happen until finally they had no choice but to spank that bad kid to get that little one to stay in bed! The punch-line that everyone would laugh about, and I mean they would really laugh hard, is that after that bad kid gets spanked and sent back to bed he gets out of bed again. His parents asked why and, that bad little kid shure has some attitude because as the story goes the child puts his hands on his tiny hip and says "it's because you didn't make me hard enough."

Later in life this kid attempted to be emancipated through the court.

When Jesus told Athena the story, she immediately recognized the gaslighting that was going on by Christian's parents. She told Jesus no kid would ever say that. She then goes on to point out the fact that the story was made up or a delusion and then also the license that Christians parents felt they had to beat their child after such an interaction. If the child kept getting up out of bed there was a reason other than the kid wanted to be beaten. That kid may have been trying to take a breath because he/she had something to say other than 'beat me harder.'

Trading Privilege for POWER

TRILOGY

BOOK III

My Life Matters

By
Joseph G. Black

Chapter 1

New Future

"Welcome to Neom", said Joe Galt. "Let us remember, That we are in the holy presence of God.

I remember the earliest podcasts with Christian and Jesus. Christian was dealing with all this new information about his family and his rights as a Beneficiary and his Pastor-Father's and Trustee Fiduchary duty while at the same time making enough to pay the bills as a car salesman. The knowledge and self confidence Jesus and Athena gave him along with divine province led him to making 2 more life changing decisions.

The 2 events change Christian' path. seeing people he knew and loved at The White House talk'n about how cool it is President Trump gave Mr. D, pardon days after meeting with the FBI because he had him in my heart during this meeting. It was difficult for me to do but I knew greater men have borne this and more.

Number two, when I planned to publish my book on my birthday, it turned out that it was Yom Kippur. I knew I had to rewrite the book, and be about forgiveness and Divine Providence.

Christian realizes after talking to Lu Ann and listening to Jesus that she is not where he should invest any more time or energy. She is a projection of his ideal woman as seen through the very damaged lens that is his broken heart. Christian was so damaged and hurt he was in his lower feminine energy and was attracting damaged women who wanted to be feminine but were operating in a lower masculine energy. This attraction is strong and can inspire but if they get together they will burn each other up.

Christian began to believe in himself and stepped into his masculinity thanks to Jesus. He was abused for years by his family who brought up the way they would livestock. He always had food and shelter but so do lambs and goats intended for slaughter.

Christian was inspired by Lu Ann. Jesus loved him and he was informed by Athena. He once again believed in his ability and his self worth.

He believes now that his life matters. Because Christian's life matters he forgave and moved on but also crowdfunded the damages. Christian was made whole by forgiving and by giving the public the chance to see his side of his story and participate in what he believed was the right thing; he had further evidence that the world is full of good rational people. Every action has an equal and opposite reaction. He would not bring a lawsuit against his birth family. Especially if it meant they could face a possible 30 year sentence in federal prison. At their age this would almost certainly be a life sentence. It is only appropriate that after he stands up for himself that he starts looking out for everyone else. This is why he only secondarily decided to ask the world to be a better place to live. For myself first. And also the rest of us.

The moral of the story: you're amazing. You can do it. You're the incredible you! You don't need lawyers and the DOJ in most cases you can choose to free yourself and live free. Trade your **Privilege** for **Power** by just giving up the person you thought you were and become the authentic you.

Christian went on to have many entertaining podcasts with Jesus. One I'll never forget was when he started talking about how he thinks the trinity needs either a gay man or a loving woman figure. Jesus couldn't believe what he was hearing. Christian went on to talk about how this could be a simulation and if so you may be the only one here in this reality which is just your head space and therefore because you may be a woman or a gay man and you may be the only one here that makes sense if thats who you are and that helps you relate to the almighty. Once again Jesus could hardly believe what he was hearing. He was sort-of agreeing with it. Or the time Christian asks Jesus why Yeshua is always doing that power pose in the statues like he is trying to manifest his own positive self image. That was too funny in a messed up way. Christian brought up some other more serious points to Jesus like the podcast where he is asking Jesus if about how in ther bible before Yeshua is crucified he talks about how he will come back and then well after he is crucified to death he comes back 3 days later and has new powers.... So what are we waiting for here? A threepete perhaps? Didn't we already have the second coming? Why are we still waiting?

Christian used to talk about the Highest duty one can owe another under the law as. This is a Fiduciary duty and a lot of people don't know about it just like Christian before his discovery. This is a duty that if owed means you have to put that person's interests before your own. You cannot take a deal for yourself that you wouldn't take for your person you owe this duty to. For instance...
You must put the beneficiary of the trust relationship that exists in this relationship first.

Christian went on to talk about forgiveness a lot as well and how the path the heaven is Love and Forgiveness. This is why we are not here on earth alone. We are all put here for the good of others like Marcus Arilus says in Meditations. Love... transgression and debt and... we have been taught how to deal with this too. Forgiveness and knowledge of the divinity that is in all of us. That divine providence that is within and without and all around.

One of my favorites was when Christian started off about Constantine! Talk'n about how he must have created the second heaven on earth. Talk'n bout his empire lasted 1,000 years just as described in the book of the Revelation of John and their wealth was so great they basically had streets of gold metaphor speaking thanks to the trade that happened through the stratification placement of the city. This was a golden era for the people of the earth living in this kingdom. He just thought the New Heaven is the Neo-Flavian era and the first heaven and first earth is the Flavian era. The lands beyond the roman command of the house of Flavious was the first earth. He says this is why that empire adopted the bible. This empire took place after the second coming and was the second heaven while the times of Marcus Arilus was the times of the first heaven. Jesus listened to all this patiently and lovingly. Christian was talk'n 'bout how this is why we're so confused. It's because we don't know who we are, we don't know where we are much less when we are.

Did you hear about the time Christian askes Steve Young and Jerry Rice to "keep it down please" because he was in the next room trying to sleep and they're playing Madden Football in the very next room? It seemed like a normal request for a 10 year old to make. And so it was. He had school and was always a 2 sport student athlete. A group was at coach Mike Holgram's house for a team dinner and Christian and his family was staying the night there and it was past my bedtime. The Pro-Football Hall of Fameers were polite and said "ok buddy, sorry about that!" They must have thought the whole thing was too funny. Thinking about it the funniest part is the fact that it was so unexpected. Why wouldn't a 10 year old?...

This life we live isn't a Race. Teams work together for each other and when one wins all win. When all win the individual wins.

Not all the podcast stories Chrisrtian told were as happy, in fact some were strange but it doesn't matter. He and Mr. J had custody of his money under the power of attorney and unfortunately, for Christian, this lasted until he hired a legal team capable of… very capable.

That doesn't make sense but of course a lot about his childhood and into his adulthood, under the control of the Power Of Attorney, which overlapped from his childhood by 6 months and lasted almost 20 years, did. Beyond weird and moving to down right disappointing was listening to Christian talking about the time he was at the Arizona Biltmore with Mother and Pastor-Father listening to him talk about the once in a lifetime opportunity he had and barley missed because of a scheduling conflict. He had the Once In A Lifetime Opportunity conduct an offsite on Teamwork in the most spectacular place. He went on to tell me about this Beautiful hotel built right into the side of the mountain and how amazing this place he was invited to as if he was bragging. Christian listened with disbelief. He was frozen for just a moment in time. "Bamf Canada?" Asked Christian. Pastor-Father is amazed his only son knows about this place and is like yes, that's the place and asks how he knows about this one of a kind little jem. Christian was more upset here than I have toe words to explain. He says his sweet highschool girlfriend and her family had invited him to go with them to this hotel after he graduated from De La Salle. Pastor-Father said no! It was immoral and so Christian stayed home doing nothing. He was angry but his Pastor-Father told him to trust him. He was doing this for the best. He was the one who convinced the attornies to give him the access to the award money only because Pastor-Father was going to be the Trustee. His girl and their family was in Bamf Canada and Christian was home with mother and Pastor-Father living in this 2 bedroom million dollar town house they rented. He had to sleep in the garage because my younger sister was a freshman in High School and had the other room. There among all the Privileges of a prince of Pro-Fotball at the League meetings Christian had a dificult moment and truth to confront looking at his Pastor-Father. He justified his action or lack of action all those years ago. What action could he have taken over a man who had control of my newly found fortuan and held that over his head to control him. This is Hell. I CAN'T BREATH.

Live Yeshua in our hearts forever.

That is how I remember every podcast ending between Jesus and Christian.

Chapter 2

Don't Pee on me and Tell Me It's Raining

███████████████████████ Phone Number ████
███████████████████████ Fax Number ████
███████████████████████

November 6, 2019

Via Electronic Mail to ████████████

Via Certified Mail RRR: ████████████
████████████
ATTN ████████████
████████████
████████████

    Re: REPLY TO YOUR OCTOBER 17, 2019 REQUEST
            FOR RECORDS REGARDING ████████████

████████

    Our firm, ████████████ represents ████████████ regard to the above referenced matter. Accordingly, you may direct communications concerning this matter to the undersigned.

Request for Information – ███████
Page 2 of 3

We have received and reviewed your letter to ███████ and ███████ October 17, 2019. (the "Letter"). As both of our clients are ███████, I will refer to ███████ and ███████ solely for the sake of clarity, by their first names.

While our firm does not represent ███████ and we are unaware at this time if he is represented by counsel regarding this matter, we do know that ███████ has never had a power of attorney concerning ███████ nor has he ever exerted or maintained any care or control over ███████ r his finances. As you may be aware, ███████ invested approximately $8,500 in the aggregate in ███████ nergy, through ███████ Partners a company with whom ███████ is a partner. ███████████████████████████████████████ invested came directly from ███ and ███████ own money provided by them to ███████ so that ███████ could make investments in the future should he desire). These investments by ███████ ere made on his own accord starting in 2006 when ███████ as 21 years old and was fully aware of the potential risks of his investment. ███████ Energy has not materialized, at this time, into the financial success that ███████ and countless others had hoped for, asserting that Mr. ███████ omehow had a fiduciary duty to ███████ due to ███████ investment ███████ Energy would be misplaced if asserted. This is simply my opinion because as previously stated, I do not represent Mr. ███████ and am not authorized to speak on Mr. ███████ behalf on this or any other matter.

As to ███████ ve do not contest ███████ duty as a fiduciary to ███████ pursuant to the power of attorney issued regarding ███████ s finances and are 100% confident that ███████ faithfully and appropriately served in this capacity meeting and even exceeding the fiduciary standard to which he was held. ███████ will gladly provide any and all documents requested in your Letter that are in his possession or that he can reasonably obtain. Keep in mind, however, that many of the records that you are requesting are from between 2002 and 2008, so obtaining said records to the extent they are not currently in ███████ possession may take some time. ███████ has already started the process of gathering any such records that he can and we will provide them to you as they become available. To the extent any such records are not available t ███████ or must be requested by ███████ directly as the account

Request for Information
Page 3 of 3

holder, we will advise you of the same so that you can assist ▇ in obtaining those records directly. Again, we will freely provide to you the documents that we possess or can obtain a ▇ has nothing to hide.

Obviously, it is deeply concerning to ▇ as a father that ▇ believes or may believe that ▇ as done anything inappropriate financially regarding ▇ settlement funds. Again while we are confident that the records will clearly reflect the same, we can only hope that these efforts resolve this matter for ▇ sake not only legally, but personally as well and that ▇ and ▇ can take the steps to start to heal this obviously strained father-son relationship. I look forward to working with you in the coming months to amicably resolve this matter for our respective clients. Should you have any questions, please feel free to contact me directly.

                                            Very truly yours,

cc: ▇ (Sent Via Email)

Chapter 3

Hustle Harder Hustle Smarter

Curtis Jackson explains nothing can beat the heart of a

Hustler. Also talks about betrayal by the people who are supposed to love you and how that is the worst thing to go through.

THIS PAGE LEFT BLANK INTENTIONALLY

Chapter 4

podcast

JOE GALT SAYS, "LET US REMEMBER:

THAT WE ARE IN THE HOLY PRESENCE OF GOD."

Jesus and Athena stay with me here at the beech home which is nice like The Breakers Palm Beach or the place in the mountains which is nice like Bamf by the way. I havent see LuAnn here but I sure do remember meeting her. Jesus talks about how he convinced Christian to write out his thoughts and feelings by playing a psychological trick on him. This is why I love Jesus so much. He used the inspiration and motivation Christian had to get closer. The writing he did was not for her it was for him. He got to understand who he was like looking in a mirror by writing to someone. Also LuAnn gets drunk and that's why Jesus insisted he write her letters. He convinced Christian she would remember what he told her however to be honest half the time Christian was drunk to remember what he told her. Pen and paper create a reference to go back to and allowed Christian to review who he is becoming and what is really important. Christian and Jesus and Athena are are enjoying the beauty of Neom as they tell Joe Galt about another Podcast. They wanted his take on the matter Christian brought up asking if God/YahWay Yeshoua's lower self? Is that his past self? Who he used to be? Maybe that is why he calls him The Father. We used to be our father if you think about it. So then the way it relates to us as a microcosm of everything The Father is Alone and Cruel sometimes and if Yeshua our present self and is the Savior are we given the opportunity to be the holy spirit when we work together? Jesus asked Christian if he just create God in my own image returning the favor in a tone that made light of the comment. Joe Galt asked Who is the almighty and why is his name I AM?

Christian was going through the most difficult part of the discovery, about the same time, the podcast happened. That can't be a coincidence said Joe Galt. So after hiring the most amazing legal team and gathering information for a civil lawsuit, they tell him it's gotta go through a criminal court first? And so you go and meet with the FBI just like that? Because you thought they had spent Christian's money overseas in Australia, and that vacation was paid for with money given for his head injury I see. And then, three days later you see The best wide receiver to ever play the game at the White House grateful to be there and grateful for the president United States, giving Mr. D a pardon! And you took that as a sign from the Almighty. My God! I guess he got into some trouble, but he's a pretty good guy and the party was in the best interest of the public. Otherwise the president of United States wouldn't be messing around with it. Maybe that's why the people at the FBI were so concerned with Christian story, and gave him so much of their time and attention, which he sure thought was strange at the time, and it only made sense after seeing the part, and that was handed down realizing that the agency was speaking with, must've been aware this was about to happen. I spoke to Christian in such a kind and informative way, and it was more like two friends talking then it was anything else. Unlike a hired attorney looking for a commission and a big windfall these guys, Christian felt like we're shooting him straight. It restored his faith in humanity in someway, and he took their advice to heart. Later in that podcast, Christian and Jesus were talking about how his Pastor-Father was at every Football Practice watching me not working. While we had no savings or money for anything but the bear necessities of life. He also coached Christian and his 2 sisters baseball and softball team every year while everyone else's mother and father was working. He was always watching us and wanted us to love nobody else. He wanted our love all to himself. Premarital sex was the worst thing we could do or anything that could lead to this. He wanted our mind, body and soul and would get violently angry if we refused him. I'm sure he thought this was the godly thing and the right thing to do from where he stood but it sure was difficult for me and must've been for my other sister who try to be emancipated at one point.

Joe doesn't have anything to say about that. Another podcast around this time of Christian's discovery they covered the topic how every action has an equal and opposite reaction and that if someone does you wrong maybe something happens for them but what will happen for you is an equal and opposite reaction. If you forgive them, that is a further action that will create an equal and opposite reaction so vengeance is mine, says the lord, forgive and move on, just like the president for gave Mr. D, Christian decided to forgive pastor, father, mother, and Mr. J.

We live in a fair simulation. People get what they deserve. This golden rule was given to us in a specific time and specific place for a certain reason. Liberty and freedom will always have their place amount tyrants and robber barons.

Christian was so hurt by his father mother and projected God the father in that same light so I think that's what led him to ask on the next podcast if Yah-Way was the god of Caninan, Ball or moloch? Because in Waco he realized he had been dealing with a cult of people who dealt in human sacrifice and used cannibalism as a central point of their religion.

Live Yeshua in our hearts forever. Athena talked to Jesus about this podcast because it reminded her of the situation she had with her ex-husband who would use his disabled son's money to buy dinners for the three of them sometimes which seems reasonable in some ways just like taking your whole family to Australia may seem reasonable, even if it was for money designated for Christian, who had had a jury and a disability. Yes Christian got some benefit for it but so did everyone else, and they didn't have the same circumstances in special needs that Christian had.

Chapter 5

FINAL WORDS

Gmail

Important email
14 messages

Tue, Oct 8, 2019, 1:58 PM

To:
Bcc:

I have a few questions:

Is there a power of Attorny agreement between us and if so could I please see it.

If there is not a POA how were you able to spend my money as you pleased.

Do you think it was ok to tell me that I needed to pay for my Sr. Year of high school at De La Salle?

Did you steal that money from me and use it for your Benefit? Did you abuse your position of authority as my father, pastor who baptized me, and power of attorny?

I trusted you to help me make good financial decisions with that money. I believed and trusted you and ▓▓ would help me and not hurt me.

Why would you advise me to invest in ▓▓ Energy instead of MSFT or real estate? Was that because you could use your position as my POA and high net worth to get yourself a foot into ▓▓ and possibly make yourself rich? Was it not for my position in ▓▓ Energy would you have been allowed to have one pre IPO?

How were you able to simultaneous send my two sisters to college while at the same time not able to send me through college while at the same time being my POA and using my money to send me through school.

Did you steal that money from me and use it for what you wanted to use it for?

Were you able to pay for my sisters education because you had access to that money?

Did you personally benefit from your position of trust I gave you with that money.

Do you think it was wrong for you to not give up your role as POA when that trust was broken after only one semester at Baylor and I told you I didn't want you to manage the money any more?

I realized after my first semester that I couldn't trust you to have my best interest in mind because it turned out you moved to a house where I did not have a room to sleep in and you were paying for Dr. Steinberg out of my money not yours which I was not expecting. $500/hr. I wanted to have total

access to the money and have you off my account so I could invest in Microsoft and real estate and not go broke. I wanted to make my money last. Why did you think it was ok to not give me what was mine?

Was it because of my learning disability that you felt it necessary to not let me have access to my money?

If so why did you have access to it instead of a POA who would act in my best interests.

On a very personal note I would like for you to know the permanent damage that is caused when trusting someone with their personal finances and that person uses the money for himself or pretends to. At least a dozen times I saw you pretend to pay for expensive items such as a family dinner with my credit card. To this day I don't understand that other than it was a way of making light of something that was being done in private without me knowing. You thought it was funny. It made me sick. Maybe you just wanted me to know you had your foot on my neck and could do whatever you wanted and there was nothing I could do about it.

again all the while you think it's fun and funny. It was not. And it was not funny to pretend to spend my money. I didn't consent to ▇▇▇▇▇▇ and I didn't consent to you spending my money or having any access to it after my freshmen year of Baylor.

You told me you needed to borrow money from me to start Sports Leadership Group. I would like to know exactly how much of my money was used for that.

I would like to see exactly how much of my money was invested into both ▇▇▇ energy as well as Sports Leadership Group. Or did you just basically have a quarter million dollar pot to take from as you pleased while you were starting your consulting company.

It's unfortunate that I have had to carry this around all these years but when ▇▇▇ told me I would get every penny back I originally got from the lawsuit once ▇▇▇ went public I believed him. Therefore it seemed to me there was no real loss of money if ▇▇▇ had a separate account with all that money in it or much more. How could I be that mad if you did what was best for me. Only now after the IPO can I see this was not the case.

Do you have any intention of paying me back the money you took from me or paying me unpaid dividends and equity in your company started with my misappropriated capital you had access to?

[Quoted text hidden]

Tue, Oct 8, 2019, 7:25 PM

I received your email today.
You have many important questions and thoughts.
I would like some time to consider everything you have asked and said.
I will respond in the next few days.
[Quoted text hidden]

Tue, Oct 15, 2019, 3:31 PM

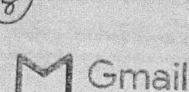 

Gmail

Reply to your important email
4 messages

Thu, Oct 10, 2019, 11:25 AM

Thank you for writing this email. While it may have been difficult, it is important.

There are many things here that I'd like to understand better. These have obviously caused you pain and sorrow.

When you received the money from the lawsuit you trusted me to help you with the stewardship of that money for your benefit. You also trusted ▆▆ to invest some of that money in Bloom.

You sensed that I used my authority and position with POA to benefit myself and perhaps your sisters. This resulted in you losing trust in me and questioning if I had your best interest in mind.

I imagine the sense that I betrayed you would be very deep, and of course very damaging.

The serious failure of the ▆▆ investment, coupled with the other areas when you sensed I mis-spent your money, is only made worse by the sense that I made light of the situation. The handling of someone else's money is very serious. If you thought I took that lightly it makes sense that you would feel betrayed and hurt.

You have carried these burdens quite a while.

I answer your questions below, but first I just wanted to check to see I'm understanding you.

Is the above correct or am I missing something?

I have a few questions:

I'm very sorry for the pain this has caused you. I hope this information can be of some help to you.

Is there a power of Attorny agreement between us and if so could I please see it.
Yes there is, I'm glad to mail it to you if you wish.

If there is not a POA how were you able to spend my money as you pleased.

send me through college while at the same time being my POA and using my money to send me through school.

- She worked two jobs
- She took out loans
- We also had donors that helped pay for about two years of her tuition
- We also took out a partial loan

- She worked two jobs
- She took out loans
- She earned a partial scholarship
- We took out a partial loan

Did you steal that money from me and use it for what you wanted to use it for?

Never

Were you able to pay for my sisters education because you had access to that money?

No. We took out loans and paid it out of our own small ministry salary.

Did you personally benefit from your position of trust I gave you with that money.

No. I took great care to pay your personal credit card bill on time, your tuition, room, meals, and to move money from your Brokerage Account to checking only when you needed it.

Do you think it was wrong for you to not give up your role as POA when that trust was broken after only one semester at Baylor and I told you I didn't want you to manage the money any more?

We discussed it. But we did agree to keep the arrangement of me paying your bills out of your money so you could focus on school.

I realized after my first semester that I couldn't trust you to have my best interest in mind because it turned out you moved to a house where I did not have a room to sleep in and you were paying for Dr. Steinberg out of my money not yours which I was not expecting. $500/hr.

We moved to a two-bedroom condo because it was the best we could afford at that time. We felt very badly there wasn't a room for you. I don't remember what Dr Steinberg charged, it was a lot, but I don't think it was that high. I could be wrong though.

I wanted to have total access to the money and have you off my account so I could invest in Microsoft and real estate and not go broke. I wanted to make my money last. Why did you think it was ok to not give me what was mine?

Your money was only spent on your needs and expenditures.

Do you think it was ok to tell me that I needed to pay for my Sr. Year of high school at De La Salle?

For three years Mom and I paid for DLS with some need-based scholarship you got from DLS. After your award, the scholarship money was not available, it seemed reasonable to us that you could pay tuition for Sr year out of your award.

Did you steal that money from me and use it for your Benefit?

No

Did you abuse your position of authority as my father, pastor who baptized me, and power of attorny?

Ultimately you will be the judge of that, but I never believed I did.

I trusted you to help me make good financial decisions with that money. I believed and trusted you and Brent would help me and not hurt me.

Of course. We appreciated your trust and never wanted to do anything but help you.

Why would you advise me to invest in Bloom Energy instead of MSFT or real estate?

The vast majority of money was invested in a brokerage managed account. That account did quite well your freshman year. The returns covered the cost of your freshman year tuition if I remember correctly. Only a small amount of your money was invested in ▇▇▇ It seemed like a reasonable amount.

Was that because you could use your position as my POA and high net worth to get yourself a foot into BE and possibly make yourself rich?

▇▇▇ invited me to invest. I did not need your investment to get me in.

▇▇▇ and ▇▇▇ pu▇▇▇▇ his own money in for mom and me so we hopefully could retire one day.

Was it not for my position in ▇▇▇ Energy would you have been allowed to have one pre IPO?

As I said above, we all went in as "friends and family" of ▇▇▇ No money minimums were required. Your investment was not required for me to get in. Nor was my investment required for you to get in. Being friends of ▇▇▇ as the only requirement.

How were you able to simultaneous send my two sisters to college while at the same time not able to

2 bd   2 ba   1,436 sqft
2158 Myrtle Beach Ln, Danville, CA 94526
Sold: $925,000   Sold on 07/01/19   Zestimate®: $937,812
Est. refi payment: $4,960/mo   See current rates

Home value   Owner tools   Home details   Neighb ›

Is this your rental?

Get a monthly local market report with comparable rentals in your area.

○ I own and manage this rental

COMP

2 bd | 2 ba | 1,436 sqft

631 Silver Lake Dr, Danville, CA 94526

● **Off market**

Zestimate®: **$1,119,700**   Rent Zestimate®: $3,900

Est. refi payment: $7,079/mo

$ Refinance your loan

Home value | Owner tools | Home details | Nei >

Many people, including the lawyers, thought you should not have access until 22 or 25. I decided you were mature enough to have access and I knew you wanted to invest the money, so it was my decision to let you have access to the money.

Was it because of my learning disability that you felt it necessary to not let me have access to my money?

No, you're smart. That's why I didn't want it to go into a trust fund that you could not have access to.

If so why did you have access to it instead of a POA who would act in my best interests.

We agreed to this arrangement together

On a very personal note I would like for you to know the permanent damage that is caused when trusting someone with their personal finances and that person uses the money for himself or pretends to.

I know there is great damage from all this. I'm very, very sorry for that.

At least a dozen times I saw you pretend to pay for expensive items such as a family dinner with my credit card. To this day I don't understand that other than it was a way of making light of something that was being done in private without me knowing. You thought it was funny. It made me sick. Maybe you just wanted me to know you had your foot on my neck and could do whatever you wanted and there was nothing I could do about it.

I would not make fun of you. I don't believe I ever bought a meal with your money. I do remember buying sheets and supplies for your dorm room at Target with your money. You were with us when that happened. There was never a thought of controlling you, we always wanted you to be a mature, independent person

again all the while you think it's fun and funny. It was not. And it was not funny to pretend to spend my money. I didn't consent to ▇▇▇ and I didn't consent to you spending my money or having any access to it after my freshmen year of Baylor.

I have expressed my regret for ▇▇▇ apologize for that. I can tell it hurt you. I am sorry.

You told me you needed to borrow money from me to start ▇▇▇ I would like to know exactly how much of my money was used for that.

None of your money was spent on ▇▇▇ No money was needed for that ▇▇▇ didn't charge me to join. There was no need of capital from anyone.

I would like to see exactly how much of my money was invested into both ▬ energy as well as Sports Leadership Group. Or did you just basically have a quarter million-dollar pot to take from as you pleased while you were starting your consulting company.

No money was invested in Sports Leadership Group.

▬ investments were as follows

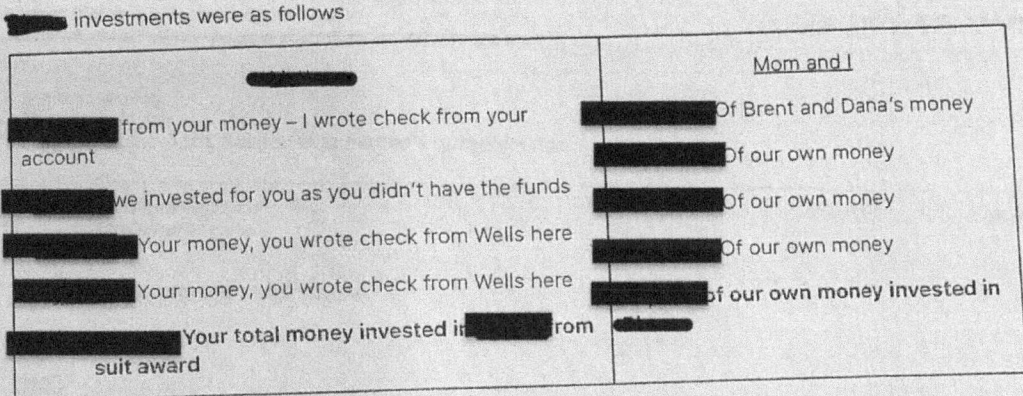

In total:

You invested ▬ of your award, your money, in ▬ Energy.

- We put $1400 of our money in your account as they required minimums to keep investing in future and you didn't have it at the time.
- We invested a total ▬ of our own money, ▬ invested another ▬ to get us started. We still have our stock; it is worth only ▬ today.

It's unfortunate that I have had to carry this around all these years but when ▬ told me I would get every penny back I originally got from the lawsuit once bloom went public I believed him. Therefore, it seemed to me there was no real loss of money if ▬ had a separate account with all that money in it or much more. How could I be that mad if you did what was best for me. Only now after the IPO can I see this was not the case.

It is unfortunate for us all. You could have invested ▬ somewhere else. ▬ turned out to be very bad for all of us.

I hope I've answered your questions. I've also attached a word doc of this email,

FOUNDER | THE SPORTS ▬
PRINCIPAL CONSULTANT ▬

Chapter 6

Determining damages for Breach of Fiduciary by Christina M. Carroll
LEGALZOOM has good information about this duty. This chapter contains blank space for the reader to write down in their own words what

they understand fiduciary duty to be.

$1,685,136.93 the amount of money Pastor Father Trustee and Mr. J had in their custody and care over the term prior to discovery.
$350,000.00 invested in the S&P 500 from 2002 - 2020 is

+$2,252,500.Unpaid dividend disgorged from Sports Consulting group. 50% of the Gross profit from the consulting company founded with Christian's money is as such. 2004-2020
Estimated total gross profit:
The first year
$10,000.
$20,000.
$60,000.
$120,000.
$200,000.
$250,000.
$240,000.
$240,000.
$300,000.
$260,000.
$350,000.
$350,000.
$400,000.
$450,000.
$410,000.
$450,000.
$395,000.

Total
$4,505,000.
Christian's unpaid dividends are half of this number.

- + $87,000.Ch13 bankruptcy of $1,450 x 60 months
- + $5,000 for Leagul fees to change name because Father Pastor and his Trustee could freely withdraw money from his account, and take out loans under his name without him being the present.
- + $850,000 Lost income due to PTSD and depression: $50,000 x 17 years

- $0 to $4,879,636.93 Emotional distress caused could be up to the monetary damage totaling: Christian was diagnosed with PTSD by Stephen Parham, Ph.D.And needed treatment for emotional distress by medical doctors for 20 years.

Between $4,879,636 and $9,759,272 actual damage.
- $48,796,360.00 to $97,592,720.00 if we went to trial. There is no cap on punitive damages that can be awarded for breach of fiduciary. It could very well be 10x actual damages. Christian had retained a legal team with a solid track record of getting this for their clients. They represented Christian well and would have brought the issue through to be DOJ first and then picked up up where they left off as a civil case. Christian was lookin at a possible case worth

$53,675,996.00 $107,351,992.00 if we aren't settled and go to a trial after Discovery through the DOJ And or IRS and any other governing agencies.

This chapter is left blank for the reader to read and draw conclusions

Chapter 7
Podcast

LET US REMEMBER:

THAT WE ARE IN THE HOLY PRESENCE OF GOD.

Questions
1. What if we changed the world by changing one word? ***RACE***
2. What if I AM the only one here??
3. If the trinity is I then is that why God the father was moving on the earth then stopped while Jesus jesus had to leave to let the greater one come. Like it's about the same person I am in my past present and divine providential form.

Stories
1. De La Salle 151 game win streak. Brotherhood Bleeding into betrayal because I believed My family could be trusted. They were in football and with god and Pastor-Father had become a consultant teaching Trust is the most important.
    a. Realizing they had my money and I could do nothing about it. They weren't part of my team like my Spartan brothers were everything is different.
    b. TK brother Murdered
    c. My True Pastor Kyle Lake electrocution on sunday morning and leaving earth in front of the whole church.

With all this going tying to make grades at Baylor in the strange town of Waco with a disability how could I sue my family for control of my money when what I really needed and didn't have wasn't money it was love and freedom.

2. Coach Mariucci after beating the arch rival handing Mr. J. the game ball because he was the closest to me and he was going to go ahead of the rest of the team to make it to my hopital bed and give me that game ball. Coach Much says after the win that were a team in here and one of us is in the hospital with a serous injury so we played great today and this game ball goes to Christian.
3. The first time Pro-Football took a knee for a cause it was not before the tame it was after. Both times it started in the great city of San Francisco. I have a vision that San Francisco and thor professional sports teams all over the bay will be among the first along with Mr. D. to take a stand and end the Human Races.

Statements

1. There is no day but today. There's only this. Only now. "This moment contains all moments." C. S. Lewis The Great Divorce "The present is the point where time touches eternity." C. S. Lewis The Screwtape Letters.
2. Forgiveness and Love line the path to heaven here in this place at this time.
    a. Great Leaders that found heaven in this place down this path
        i. Yeshua
        ii. Isaaic
        iii. Joseph
        iv. John D. Rockefeller
3. Intigraion is the third I we can use to see paradise.

Live Yeshua in our hearts forever.
Romans 12:19
This Podcast ends with the playing of the song
Brothers In Arms by Dire Straits

Chapter 8

FREEDOM

NO. 2021-47251

IN THE MATTER OF	§	IN THE DISTRICT COURT
	§	
▬▬▬▬▬▬▬▬▬▬▬▬▬	§	245th JUDICIAL DISTRICT
	§	
AN ADULT	§	HARRIS COUNTY, TEXAS

NCA
CHNAX
8C

ORDER GRANTING CHANGE OF NAME OF ADULT

On November 30, 2021 , the Court considered the Petition for Change of Name of Adult of ▬▬▬▬▬▬▬▬▬ as evidenced by their signatures on this Order, all forms, pleadings and affidavits on file with the case.

Petitioner appeared in person and through attorney of record, Travis Eaton, and announced ready.

The Court finds that it has jurisdiction of the case and ▬▬▬▬▬▬▬▬▬

The making of a record of testimony was waived with the consent of the Court.

The Court finds:

1. Petitioner is an adult.
2. Petitioner's full true name is ▬▬▬▬▬▬▬▬▬
3. Petitioner's sex is Male.
4. Petitioner's race is White.
5. Petitioner was born on ▬▬▬▬▬▬▬
6. Petitioner's driver's license numbers of any license issued within the past ten years is: Texas DL# ▬▬
7. Petitioner's Social Security number i▬▬▬▬
8. Petitioner's FBI number is ▬▬▬▬▬
9.

   c.

Order Granting Change of Name
Page 1 of 2

10. █████████████████████████████████
11. █████████████████████████████████

Code of Criminal Procedure.

12. Petitioner's change of name is in the interest or to the benefit of Petitioner and is in the interest of the public.

IT IS ORDERED that Petitioner's name is changed from ███████████████ to ███████████████.

IT IS ORDERED that all relief requested in this case and not expressly granted is denied.

SIGNED on _____.

Signed: 11/30/2021

JUDGE PRESIDING

APPROVED AS TO FORM ONLY:

████████████████████
████████████████████
████████████████████
████████████
██████████

State Bar No. ████████
Attorney for Petitioner

████████████████████████

APPROVED AS TO FORM AND SUBSTANCE:

████████████████
██████████

I, Marilyn Burgess, District Clerk of Harris County, Texas certify that this is a true and correct copy of the original record filed and or recorded in my office, electronically or hard copy, as it appears on this date.
Witness my official hand and seal of office this   January 3, 2022

Certified Document Number: ███████████████

Marilyn Burgess

Marilyn Burgess, DISTRICT CLERK
HARRIS COUNTY, TEXAS

In accordance with Texas Government Code 406.013 electronically transmitted authenticated documents are valid. If there is a question regarding the validity of this document and or seal please e-mail support@hcdistrictclerk.com

UNITED STATES BANKRUPTCY COURT
SOUTHERN DISTRICT OF TEXAS

United States Bankruptcy Court
Southern District of Texas
ENTERED
January 13, 2022
Nathan Ochsner, Clerk

In Re: Debtor

Case No.
Chapter: 13

ORDER CONFIRMING CHAPTER 13 PLAN
AND VALUING COLLATERAL PURSUANT TO 11 U.S.C. § 506

1. The Court has considered confirmation of the Debtor(s)' chapter 13 plan that was proposed on 10/28/21.

2. All objections to the plan have been withdrawn or overruled.

3. The Court has determined that the plan meets all of the requirements of §1325 of the Bankruptcy Code.

4. Notwithstanding any estimate of the amount of a general or priority unsecured claim contained in the plan or in an order of the Court, the actual amount payable on priority claims will be the Allowed Amount of the priority claim and the actual proration for distribution on general unsecured claims will be based on actual Allowed Amounts of general unsecured claims.

5. In addition to the monthly payments called for under the plan, the Debtor(s) shall contribute all non-exempt proceeds from the cause(s) or potential cause(s) of action described on Schedule B into the Chapter 13 plan for distribution to the unsecured creditors.

6. The value of the collateral for secured claims is in the amount set forth in the plan.

7. The plan is confirmed.

Signed and Entered on Docket: 1/13/22.

MARVIN ISGUR
United States Bankruptcy Judge

Chapter 9

a. YALE LAW JOURNAL

Vol. XXXI MARCH, 1922 No. 5

THE TRUST AS AN INSTRUMENT OF LAW REFORM

AUSTIN W. SCOTT

Professor of Law, Harvard University

Professor Maitland, in one of his most brilliant essays,' said:

"The idea of a trust is so familiar to us all that we never wonder at it.

And yet surely we ought to wonder. If we were asked what was the

greatest and most distinctive achievement performed by Englishmen in the field of jurisprudence I cannot think that we could have any better

answer to give than this, namely, the development from century to

century of the trust idea.

We have trust in a fiduciary relationship, just like the formal trust mentioned in the article above. Trust means Trust. in the same Race means Race until wr reffing it. It's define as a contest, and it also extends to dividing people in a hierarchy that inherently makes some winners and others losers. It's time for us to move on and take control of our language. In the words we speak because my life matters. Join me and end this race.

Chapter 10

I have seen The Count of Monte Cristo. It was worth my time. "Abbe Faria: Here is your final lesson- do not commit the crime for which you now serve the sentence. God said, Vengeance is mine.
Edmond Dantes: I don't believe in God.
Abbe Faria: It doesn't matter. He believes in you."

This book was meant to be released october 5th 2022, my birthday. As the date approached I found it just so happened that this was the day of atonement this year…Yom Kippur.

For the second time The Almighty speaks to me loud and clear.

I am giving a pardon to Pastor Father and my Trustee. You are nothing more to me than Don King is to Mike Tyson. Mother and Mr. J. Are suspect but forgiven.

When something bad happens
you have three choices. You can
either let it define you, let is
destroy you, or you can let it
strengthen you.
Dr. Seuss

Christian and Lu Ann are the past lower self.
-Distorted

Jesus and Athena are the true present self. They are the children or the newer improved versions of their past self. -Defined.

Joe Galt and Chi Rho are the future. Integrated to who they were and are and they know where they're going.

-Strengthened.

I'm gonna enjoy the rest of my life and be happy. For so long I felt so blackmailed like if I was happy my Trustee pointed a finger at me and said look you're happy! What's the problem? Stop complaining about the money I have. you've got good looks got good intelligence and you're not poor so sit down and shut up! I tried to be happy but even still I felt guilty for being happy because my Trustee would tell people details like I was happy and everything's fine everything's good. Now looking at what I see to be an easy summary judgment I decide I will not commit the crime for which I now serve the sentence. Even if I am owed damages I will not take them by force. It is wrong to take somebody's property against their will. It feels beautiful to forgive. I am blessed and happier as a bankrupt carsales salesman than many rich people. I am free.

Give us this day our daily bread. And forgive us our trespasses, as we forgive those who trespass against us. And lead us not into temptation; but deliver us from evil.

Epilog 1

Anyway

People are often unreasonable, illogical and self centered;
Forgive them anyway.

If you are kind, people may accuse you of selfish, ulterior motives;
Be kind anyway.

If you are successful, you will win some false friends and some true enemies;
Succeed anyway.

If you are honest and frank, people may cheat you;
Be honest and frank anyway.

What you spend years building, someone could destroy overnight;
Build anyway.

If you find serenity and happiness, they may be jealous;
Be happy anyway.

The good you do today, people will often forget tomorrow;
Do good anyway.

Give the world the best you have, and it may never be enough;
Give the world the best you've got anyway.

You see, in the final analysis, it is between you and your God;
It was never between you and them anyway.

Epilog 2

New Heaven and New Earth

Revelation 21

Now I saw a new heaven and a new earth, for the first heaven and the first earth had passed away. Also there was no more sea. **2** Then I, [a]John, saw the holy city, New Jerusalem, coming down out of heaven from God, prepared as a bride adorned for her husband. **3** And I heard a loud voice from heaven saying, "Behold, the tabernacle of God *is* with men, and He will dwell with them, and they shall be His people. God Himself will be with them *and be* their God. **4** And God will wipe away every tear from their eyes; there shall be no more death, nor sorrow, nor crying. There shall be no more pain, for the former things have passed away."

5 Then He who sat on the throne said, "Behold, I make all things new." And He said [b]to me, "Write, for these words are true and faithful."

6 And He said to me, "It[c] is done! I am the Alpha and the Omega, the Beginning and the End. I will give of the fountain of the water of life freely to him who thirsts. **7** He who overcomes [d]shall inherit all things, and I will be his God and he shall be My son. **8** But the cowardly, [e]unbelieving, abominable, murderers, sexually immoral, sorcerers, idolaters, and all liars shall have their part in the lake which burns with fire and brimstone, which is the second death."

[VALJEAN]

Forgive me all my trespasses

And take me to your glory

[FANTINE]

Take my hand

I'll lead you to salvation

Take my love

For love is everlasting

[FANTINE & THE BISHOP]

And remember

The truth that once was spoken

To love another person

Is to see the face of God

Epilog 3

Invitation to end racism. The end of The Human Races

Do you hear the people sing

Lost in the valley of the night?

It is the music of a people

Who are climbing to the light.

For the wretched of the earth

There is a flame that never dies.

Even the darkest night will end

And the sun will rise.

They will live again in freedom

In the garden of the Lord.

They will walk behind the plough-share,

They will put away the sword.

The chain will be broken

And all men will have their reward.

Will you join in our crusade?

Who will be strong and stand with me?

Somewhere beyond the barricade

Is there a world you long to see?

Do you hear the people sing?

Say, do you hear the distant drums?

It is the future that they bring

When tomorrow comes!

Will you join in our crusade?

Who will be strong and stand with me?

Somewhere beyond the barricade

Is there a world you long to see?

Do you hear the people sing?

Say, do you hear the distant drums?

It is the future that they bring

When tomorrow comes...

Tomorrow comes!

The book ends like a De La Salle chapple. Offering the sign of peace intentions and a song.

And the same way Christian wrote Lu Anne a whole notebook of letters. I'm writing this entire book for myself.

I'm half way through a 60 month Ch. 13 Bankruptcy where I'm paying 100% of my debt through the court. The fundraiser will be up to the term of my bankruptcy, but trustee will be the first to receive any money given as it is my obligation through the United States Court. All are welcome to participate. I'm half way through a 60 month Ch. 13 Bankruptcy where I'm paying 100% of my debt through the court. The fundraiser will be up to the term of my bankruptcy, but trustee will be the first to receive any money given as it is my obligation through the United States Court. All are welcome to participate.

gofundme.com/give-money-that-was-taken-by-father-pastor

The End

Made in the USA
Coppell, TX
01 May 2024

31892064R00098